DATE DUE

NOV 30 '79

DEMCO 38-297

the Joy of Building

RESTORING THE CONNECTION BETWEEN ARCHITECT AND BUILDER

Forrest Wilson

VNR VAN NOSTRAND REINHOLD COMPANY

NEW YORK   CINCINNATI   TORONTO   LONDON   MELBOURNE

Copyright (c) 1979 by Litton Educational Publishing, Inc.

Library of Congress Catalog Card Number 78-31710

ISBN 0-442-29521-9

Printed in United States of America

Published in 1979 by Van Nostrand Reinhold Company
A division of Litton Educational Publishing, Inc.
135 West 50th Street, New York, N.Y. 10020, U.S.A.

Van Nostrand Reinhold Limited
1410 Birchmount Road
Scarborough, Ontario MIP 2E7, Canada

Van Nostrand Reinhold Australia Pty. Ltd.
17 Queen Street
Metcham, Victoria 3132, Australia

Van Nostrand Reinhold Company Limited
Molly Millars Lane
Wokingham, Berkshire, England

16 15 14 13 12 11 10 9 8 7 6 5 4 3 2 1

Library of Congress Cataloging in Publication Data

Wilson, Forrest, 1918-
   The joy of building.

   Bibliography: p.
   Includes index.
   1. Architecture and society. 2. Technology--
Social aspects. I. Title.
NA2543.S6W54   720'.1   78-31710
ISBN 0-442-29521-9

107586

Contents

CHoIcE ChoICe ChOIcc CHoxcE CHoIce choIcE
cHoIce ChoIcE c.OIcE CHoze chOICE .HoIcE
CHOIce ChoICE cHoIcE CHoIDc CHoICe ChoIce
CHoIce ChOICe CHoIcE cHOIcE CHDiCe CHOIcw
CHOIce ChoIce ChoICE cHoIcE cHoIce CHoxCE
ChoIce CHoIce chOIce cHOIc CHoIcE ChOIce
CHoICc cHoICE ChOIce ChoICe CHoIcE
cHoICc chDIce CHoICE CHoIcE Chcoice

NOTRE DAME OF PARIS (Courtesy of French Tourist Office)

McDONALD'S TWIN TRIUMPHAL ARCHES   Route 1, College Park, Maryland

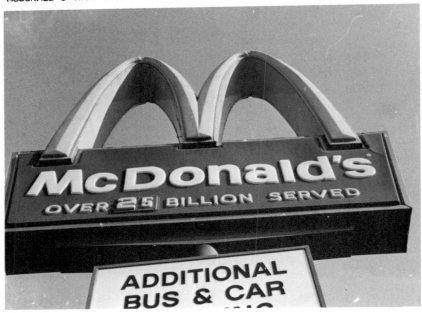

Introduction

None of the great architectural styles of the past was ever inspired by the aesthetic frivolity attributed to their builders by architectural historians.

Architectural styles or points of view are the by-products of emerging patterns of ideas that come in conflict with existing patterns of thought. An example is the emergence of the building form we have come to know as the Gothic style which is attributed to the abbot Suger for the rebuilding of the Romanesque church at Saint Denis during the mid-twelfth century. In any other than an architectural history, it can be clearly seen that the method of building employed at Saint Denis had very little to do at all with architectural style or theory or aesthetics as we know them. Suger ingeniously brought together a number of structural innovations prevalent at the time and combined them into an integral whole, which historians have dubbed "the beginnings of the Gothic style."

Such frivolity was not the good abbot's intent. Politically, Suger was a very powerful man. He was counsellor to two of the most vigorous kings of France and served as leading regent when one went on a crusade. The kings Suger served so well were assembling a nation minced by English invasions, papal antagonisms, and warring baronies and fiefdoms. The symbol of Gothic style, the Gothic arch, served the same purpose then as McDonald's golden arches serve today. It symbolized chopped ingredients brought into a palatable whole. For McDonald's it is the hamburger; for Suger, the emergence of a national state.

Three centuries later, architectural historians claim, Leon Battista Alberti inaugurated Renaissance architecture with a commission awarded to him by Sigismondo Malatesta, lord of Rimini. Historians neglect to mention that Sigismondo was a tyrant and occasional <u>conditiere</u>. Conditiere, as leaders of bands of mercenary soldiers, were the hit men of Renaissance Italy. Alberti was instructed to remodel the thirteenth-century Gothic church of San Francesco into a memorial to Sigismondo to improve his image. Alberti borrowed an earlier successful trademark from Roman antiquity, the motif of the triumphal arch, to symbolize his client's victory over death. But all was to no avail; Sigismondo died before the church was completed and the city of Rimini was later sold to Venice. Nevertheless, this fifteenth-century public relations gesture has persisted in architectural histories as the beginning of the Renaissance style in architecture.

CONDITIERE
(after drawing
by Ucello)

TRIUMPHAL ARCH (International
Correspondence School Rendering
June 15, 1893)

Buildings are the husks that enclose new social, political, and economic relationships. When new ideas emerged, buildings of the past became cicada shells to be altered as Suger, Alberti, and countless nameless American carpenters have always done. In the doing, unique building forms are created, but these are by-products, not intentions.

What historians later identify as "stylistic perfection" is never achieved as an objective, only as a by-product. Conversely, mediocre buildings invariably appear when designed self-consciously instead of as containers of more serious intentions. Attempts today to create unique forms for bureaucratic commercial and institutional structures are adequate proof of this contention.

It seems to be the curious function of architectural historians to study cicada shells as an art form. As a result, architectural theory has reached a high level of confusion. The significance of the form is rhapsodized and the vital forces that shaped the shell ignored. On the surface this would seem as harmless an activity as working crossword puzzles or picking the daily double at the local racetrack. However, the concentration on cicada shell aesthetics has led us to an appalling mediocrity in interpreting the significance of the life that generates the form of buildings.

Our very skill in theorizing has obstructed the possibility of our learning the real significance of the act of building in the past, clouds our interpretation of the unique and vital signs of building creativity in the present, and distorts our projections of their significance as new forms that will emerge in the future.

But there is one aspect of the art of building, which was once the definition of architecture, that remains constant and that is the nature of building work itself. The ingenuity and the skill of builders, the imagination of craftsmen, and the organization of the labor force clearly mirror the life and times of each period of history. For example, we know that there is a connection between building buildings and knocking them down. All nations organize their armies for war very much as they organize their labor force for building. In the Greek and Persian Wars the Persians fought in massed ranks as they had been organized to build huge irrigation projects and mud metropolises. The Greeks, on the other hand, fought as individual soldiers, just as they build their temples, stone on stone.

Working in his studio above, Rudolph assembles the small Lego pieces, which connect with interlocking teeth, then puts all the parts together to form the largest of his models (right). It contains 35 to 40 living units in each of 11 clusters grouped around a central service core, and stands four feet high.

LIFE MAGAZINE, 1969

VOLKSWAGEN ASSEMBLY LINE (Courtesy of Volkswagen Corp.)

The mastering of gravity by physical forces, which must be achieved by builders in order for a building to stand, and the human energy that must be expended to do this does not change over time, although it takes and continues to take many different forms. Buildings stand because of human work. It is the work that concerns us here and leads us to the subject of this book.

It is proposed here that during thousands of years of building that have gone by, seldom has anything as dangerous occurred as the recent willful division of head and hand in building-work, a division as extreme as that which occurred during the building of the pyramids. It is also argued here that this division of human labor, not the aesthetic form of the pyramid or our industrial buildings, is the factor of historic significance for our time.

Toward the latter part of the nineteenth century, the introduction of industrial management forcibly separated the work of head and hand and rendered them strangers and mutually antagonistic. Tinkers, spontaneous ingenuity, craftsmanship, inventors, and dreamers have been banished from the building site. All of those who formerly left the marks of their genius and their foolishness on our built surroundings to remind us of the human presence are gone.

Today design is almost exclusively the privilege of highly trained professional designers, as omnipotent as was Imhotep, the architect of the pharaoh Zoser, who commissioned the first pyramid. Our designers decide the shape of all manufactured artifacts, from toilet bowls to cities. The parts are produced by the mindless work of the assembly line and are bolted, glued, clipped, and fastened into place by indifferent assemblers, who perform their tasks as enthusiastically as Egyptian peasants jack-assed the huge pyramid stones into place at Giseh where, incidentally, they had to build three pyramids to get one right.

This is not an original revelation. It was described and the results predicted by de Tocqueville a century and a half ago, fought by Morris and Ruskin half a century later, and continues to be politely deplored by today's guardians of the cultured taste. Despite honorable intentions and great skill, our designers invariably and unwittingly destroy the places they seek to enhance in much the same way that toddlers express their love for a newborn chick by crushing its delicate bones between their clumsy, caressing fingers. Historians and architectural theorists strive manfully to justify these efforts with magnificent color photographs captioned with blithering nonsense.

AEROSOL PAINT CAN DECORATED SUBWAY TRAIN, BROOKLYN, N.Y.
(Photo by F. Wilson)

ASSEMBLY LINE NAILING MACHINE (Courtesy of Levitt Building Systems)

Yet the situation is far from hopeless. It would be useless to dwell upon if it were. People are ninety-eight percent liquid. We cannot be compressed. The more inexorably designed into indifferent surroundings we are, the stronger the pressures within us mount to burst forth. The very artifacts that render our indifferent world indifferent contain within themselves the seeds of change. The aerosol paint can has become the medium, the cities subway trains and buildings the canvas that asserts a Kilroy presence that no amount of design or detergent can eradicate.

If we look closely we will find that far from disappearing, tinkering, puttering, and creative ingenuity have reached a high level of art. Not so long ago in the 1960s, high school students easily mastered the complexities of geodesics. They shingled their domes with discarded long-playing records. The sun fused the discs and they succeeded in designing waterproof coverings for their oddly shaped structures, a thing that most architects and no building product manufacturer had been capable of accomplishing.

Semi-illiterate Appalachian moonshiners have become superb automobile mechanics and are among the world's best race-car drivers. A spokesman for the modernized, computerized, sanitized, and rationalized Washington D.C. Metro system reports the loss of over six thousand riders a day. More accurately, this "loss" indicates the precise number of people who have outsmarted the most ingenious computer system of fare collection that our transportation designers have yet devised. Wherever an airtight system of containment has been devised, "pokehole" ventilation systems simultaneously emerge. The very perfection of the system is a challenge to bring it to human terms.

The premise put forth here is that the root cause of indifferent buildings and our deadening, repetitious surroundings is the attempted imposition of such restrictive patterns of containment. These patterns are not inevitable, but are the result of a way of thinking which we must change before it destroys us and we destroy ourselves. The art of building, in the pages that follow, is conceived simply as a unique condition of work. Concentration is not placed on the cicada shell that remains after the cicada has left. Rather, we are concerned with the life within the shell that is bursting forth, which will change the form of the future shells entirely. The seminal characteristic of this new life is the conviction that those who will suffer from design decisions have the right to influence them. This idea is restoring the connection between head and hand in amazing, strange, ingenious, and marvelous ways.

The Defiant Architect

Philip Johnson Upsets the Modernists

By Wolf Von Eckardt

Not since Le Corbusier surprised them with his chapel at Ronchamp have Modern architects been as upset as they are by Philip Johnson's recent proposal for what someone dubbed "a Chippendale skyscraper."

Ronchamp, which was dedicated in 1955, is an abstract pray-in sculpture in the Vosges mountains of France. It is also Le Corbusier's sudden, impulsive defiance of the "rational" and "functional" Cubic architecture he helped invent.

Hate it or love it (and most people who have seen it find it beautiful), you can't possibly "read" from the outside what takes place inside the building or how it is constructed. Yet, such "honest" legibility of function and structure is the canon of orthodox Modernism.

Le Corbusier, who could not get many of his legible, honest structures built, said the hell with it and de-

Cityscape

signed illegible, irrational Ronchamp. The Modern movement, that is to say 20th-century architecture, has been schizophrenic ever since — torn between Le Corbusier's romantic expressionism and Mies van der Rohe's classic functionalism.

Johnson's act of defiance is just as drastic and, in the short run, possibly just as divisive.

But in contrast to the suddenness of Le Corbusier's reversal, Johnson's was long in coming. And if Johnson's new historicism proves as popular as I think it will, the Modernists, post-Modernists, ex-Modernists and assorted stylistic schizophrenics, who now giggle derisively about the "Chippendale skyscraper" will in the long run come around and get together on a common, architectural esthetic and philosophy.

In short, I believe Johnson may well unite contemporary architecture again and lead it out of both the glass box and the concrete sculpture to a new ecumenic gentility.

The "Chippendale" is a 37-story

See CITYSCAPE, C2, Col. 1

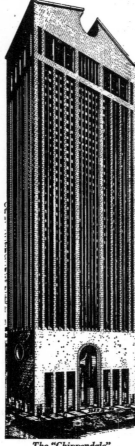

The "Chippendale"

THE WASHINGTON POST, April 22, 1978

Unfortunately, the industrial and cultural institutions that promote and further the art of building and the design and technical schools that educate practitioners have demonstrated almost no concern for this concept of simple justice, which is creating new building forms. Even though professional designers tend to ignore this phenomenon, there is no shortage of knowledgeable experts. The ability to solve building problems themselves is as common as the problems. It must be, for if we leave people and building problems undisturbed, we invariably find problem and solution emerging together.

We must conclude from this evidence that Eric Hoffer's observation is correct. Talent and genius are not rare exceptions. People are indeed, "lumpy with unrealized potentialities." The problem, as Hoffer pointed out, is that we have not yet learned how to mine these talents, but must wait for a chance to "wash nuggets out of hidden veins."

There is a history of building that could guide us, but, unfortunately, it is yet to be written. That is the story of humankind, the builder; and it would record the countless ingenious acts of creative work, which, when accumulated, make possible that one uniquely designed building that finds its way into the architectural history books. Present histories of architecture pay tribute to the final act of the architect and the cicada shell. It is as if a history of water that chronicled its transition from ice to steam were to recognize only that one degree of heat absorption that marks its change of state. In such a history we would, at sea level, laud 32 and 212 degrees Fahrenheit as degrees of genius.

We are searching for a new path and must remember that it is often easier to see the way across a stream from the other side than it is from the place it was first encountered as an obstacle. In trying to restore the connection between design and the joy of building, between the head and the hand, the cicada shell and the life within, we will, of necessity, deal primarily with found nuggets of creativity.

We will need a good deal of self-confidence to undertake such a search, for all that we find to be indifferent, deadening, and bothersome in our built surroundings apparently was the result of accident. No designer will ever declare that he or she intended to design an ugly artifact. All disclaim responsibility. Designers are to be found in the forefront of every beautification scheme and conservation effort. They serve on the boards that issue professional licenses and guide the academies that train professional designers. They serve on zoning and planning commissions and are vociferous leaders in condemning the common taste.

Help Beautify Junk Yards

THROW SOMETHING LOVELY AWAY TODAY

FRONTISPIECE PROGRESSIVE ARCHITECTURE June, 1966

So how can such a contradiction between the designer's professed beautiful intentions and the indifferent results that surround us be explained? We know that when a person says, "this is the truth," it almost certainly is a lie. If we believe in both the person and the truth, we must conclude that they are telling the truth, but using a lie to do so. In defense of truthful liars it is indeed very difficult to identify reality or truth in our changing world. Grape nuts? Who can tell the sex of a grape? Clean bombs, luxurious fallout shelters, and lung cancer riding a horse in Marlboro country makes yesterday's Dadaist pranks today's ho-hum reality.

It is no wonder that we have become strange, fay, and sometimes vicious. We must have learned this in our designed world, just as lunatics learn to be insane in asylums, for neither we nor they have had any other place to study.

Yet the incompressible human spirit always bursts forth. Irrationality breeds its own oblique creativity and nuggets of ingenious invention are found everywhere. Squatters in London usurp, repair, and make livable houses their respectable owners vandalized and abandoned. In South America, Mexico, Greece, India, Turkey, Africa, poor and often illiterate people organize and build workable houses and communities from nothing but rubble and their own energy. The spontaneous urban planning of the forgotten, as well as the do-it-yourself suburban home craftsman and housewife of industrial countries, attest to the irrepressibility of "lumpy potential."

We find that invention and ingenuity are often the most common where manufactured building materials, technology, and professional design skills are the least available. They are often richest where official government agencies ignore them or do not have the power to suppress them, for almost all creative, spontaneous design and building throughout the world seems to violate some official law, code, or ordinance and always offends the cultured taste. They also must be considered very dangerous, for within the inversion of trivia and tragedy, accident, genius, intent, and indifference, we find spontaneous building creativity labeled criminal and sometimes suppressed with troops and tanks.

Violence and building are not strangers. In the first building code ever recorded, in 2200 B. C. or thereabouts, Hammurabi stated:

If a builder build a house for a man and do not make its construction firm and the house which he has built collapse and cause the death of the owner of the house, the builder shall be put to death.

DAILY NEWS

★★★★ FINAL

Chance of showers today. High near 90. Same tomorrow. Details on page 59.

Vol. 59. No. 37   New York, Monday, August 8, 1977   Price: 20 cents

BUILDING FALLS, KILLS GIRL & DAD

6 Injured in B'klyn Collapse

News photos by Michael Lipack

Victim Ran Back To Save Daughter

Dazed and dust covered woman is carried from 34 Carroll St. (◄—) yesterday after three-story brick building collapsed, killing two. Victim Francisco Ayala, 42, escaped as house began falling apart about 4 a.m. but ran back inside crumbling structure to save daughter Marisol, 8. Both died when whole right side of building fell. Five other residents and a fireman were injured.

Stories on page 3; Other pictures in the centerfold

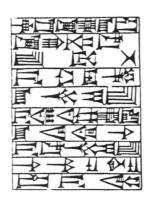

DETAIL OF HAMMURABI BUILDING CODE

As effective as Hammurabi's code may have proven to be, we can find less bloodthirsty means of accomplishing our purpose. Satire or humor is one of these. In the words of Ivan Illich:

> *Satire helps people smile moribund social systems away. Satire is adult playfulness, it is essential to purify us of our illusions. We must go beyond them if we hope to change the conditions that make them necessary. Idols must be shattered, but this is not an argument for violence. The roots of a flower grow through stone and break the stone but this is not violence.[1]*

This book is offered in the spirit of Illich's satire, rather than Hammurabi's code. The precise monotony, unresponsiveness, and machinelike simplicity that dominate life's complexity are neither monolithic nor impenetrable. The seeds of human invention, the universal will to form, the spontaneous and restless creativity, and the irresistible urge to build all find interstices between the rigid patterns imposed upon us and force them apart. For the will to form, which finds its way into the hairline cracks, grows, and eventually splits the rock apart, is as natural to humankind as is the root to trees and plants. Design, like air, is vital to all of humankind, but otherwise is unimportant.

Designer George Nelson once said that he did not believe that life was so simple that it could be transformed by a new garment of any description. Albert Einstein, Nelson noted, lived in a drab, ill-furnished, little house. Picasso had three dwellings, none of which could be accused of representing either good or contemporary design; Braque lived in a conventional Normandy farmhouse; Matisse occupied a very commonplace hotel suite. Yet all of these people were exceptionally sensitive and aware of good design.[2] As Nelson so wisely observed, design enriches its maker through the experience of creating it and can enrich the viewer equipped to respond to what it has to say. If it happens to make something easier or more comfortable, this is incidental, for a bad design could do just as well, and often does.

The design of others will not transform a human life. Only the person living the life can do so. Design reaches its full potential when it is experienced by a person fully equipped to understand and enjoy what it has to communicate. Such a person has no need of it for enrichment. This is the reason why people like Einstein and Picasso seemed to ignore its more general manifestations. They were simply busy making good design of their own and needed no further distractions.

It is proposed here that if we are to restore the connection between head and hand, design and creativity, we must recognize that not only the Einsteins, Picassos, and Braques of this world, but the Jane and John Does of the middle class and the Candy Johnsons and Juan Rodriques' of the culture of poverty have richness in their lives and are quite capable of making good designs of their own.

The works of great designers may enrich our lives if we choose to accept them, but they cannot take the place of our own creative efforts any more than others can eat, sleep, or make love in our stead. The by-product of expressing the creativity that lies in our hands as a reaction against the indifferent patterns imposed upon us and in defense of our sanity will eventually evolve a unique form of building. Let historians call it what they will.

A WORD ABOUT THE FORM OF THIS BOOK

This book is a collection of juxtaposed found ideas. It is presented as a contemporary illuminated manuscript with drawings to say things that words cannot, photographs to document things you should see for yourself, and newspaper articles as scholarly footnotes. The whole is liberally sprinkled with quotes from the common sense. It will not tell you anything you cannot see for yourself and have not seen before. It simply hopes to help you see a different pattern in reality.

footnotes

1. Ivan Illich - Interview with F. Wilson. Acapulco, Mexico, 1970.
2. George Nelson - PROBLEMS OF DESIGN, Whitney, N.Y.C., 1957 (p. 13).

SCHOOL BUILDING UNDER CONSTRUCTION (Photo by Rondal Partridge, Courtesy of SCSD Corporation)

If I did not work these worlds would perish

Bhagavad-Gita

DANGER:Men At Work

Our lives are measured by the work we do. The jobs we hold are the result of education, training, intelligence, skill, luck, and guile. Work takes the major part of the week and best part of the day and its effects live on to haunt us during sleepless nights. Work bestows or deprives us of social status; it determines where and how we live, who we shall have for friends, and how we think.

Work determines how we look and act. The walking muscles of the mailman, the sitting fat of the executive, the perpetual, forced conviviality of the used car salesman, the cynicism of the policeman, the genteel ambivalence of the architect are all occupational deformities that identify the work we do and our place in the world.

The compensation we receive for work is a measure of the society's regard for our activities, which reflects the cultural and social values of our time. It has little to do with the intrinsic human value of the work itself. The garbage man, who prevents the spread of plague, disease, and death, is neither as well compensated nor as highly regarded as the doctor, whose medical prejudices often spread more than eradicate disease.

A society classifies work in accordance with its evaluation of itself. Konrad Wachsman once said that the Renaissance could have managed without science, but not without art, and that we today can do without art, but not without science.[1] A comparison of the occupations of architecture and medicine during these two historic periods would seem to validate his statement. We know that Giotto was appointed the first Master Mason of Florence simply because he was a famous artist. He was not a mason at all.[2] Cosimo de Medici called a painter "divine," and this was the quality attributed to Michelangelo. Michelangelo agreed. Meanwhile, the science of medicine during the Renaissance was combined with barbering and hog gelding. Cardinal Richelieu, minister to the King of France, patron of the arts, and founder of the French Academy was prescribed a mixture of white wine and horse manure by his doctor on his deathbed. The man with the finest mind in Europe drank it down.[3] Today most modern statesmen do not give a damn about the paintings of Giotto or the work of Le Corbusier, but receive more medical attention for a common cold than Lorenzo the Magnificent received for all of his maladies during his entire lifetime. Science indeed seems crucial to us today, and art has little effect upon our lives.

13

TEMPLE I AND GREAT PLAZA, TIKAL
(Courtesy of the Museum of Primitive Art)

THEME BUILDING, EXPO 1967
(Courtesy of Expo Corp.)

Buildings can be built with or without scientific or artistic skill, with or without imagination, with or without inspiration, but they cannot be built without human work. Human work is the one common denominator found in all buildings. A history of the work and the work relationships of buildings would reveal a more truthful picture of architecture throughout the ages than do our present histories which are based on art.

We know, for example, that the building of New England villages was a communal, cooperative, social building project. We can tell this by the weight of the structural members; these had to have been lifted by human muscle power. We can tell by mortise, tenon, and treenail, and particularly by the dovetails of the summer beam. The system of joinery shows us that the house had to go together all at once, which would have been impossible for one or two men to accomplish. By the same token, the baloon frame of scantlings and wire nails that we find from around 1830 onward was a building of light members that could be put together, piecemeal, stick by stick, by one or two persons with a minimal amount of skill. These frame structures were erected by families in isolation on the great western prairies, after the village and community spirit of New England had disappeared from American life.

The combination of craftsmanship and technology of the buildings of the past tell us how people worked together and from this we can recreate what the society must have been like, economically, politically, and socially. What is this unique quality of work that is so vital to architecture in general and humankind in particular and that tells us so much about ourselves?

Building-work is not unique to humankind. The building ingenuity of animals and insects puts architects to shame. Bees design and build livable housing projects; man has not learned to do this. The spider is adept at building ingenious cable structures, even by Frei Otto's (the world's foremost architect of cable structures) standards, and never has a problem with material delivery. The beaver puts his tools where his mouth is and lodges where he pleases.

Creatures are loyal to their building prejudices. They select a building style and stay with it during the entire lifetime of their species. An experiment that illustrated this point was conducted with a pair of South African weaverbirds, who are members of a particularly ingenious nest-building association.

THE TRADITIONALIST

The weaverbirds were bred and rebred for five generations in the company of canaries.

They were kept out of sight and contact with their fellows and not permitted access to their usual nest-building materials. In the sixth generation of captivity, given access to the customary building materials of their species, the weaverbirds built a traditional nest correct in every detail.[4] In contrast, it is almost impossible to persuade a modern architect to design a traditional building. Obviously, human intelligence is required to design egocentrically. The distinction between the worst architect and the best insect builder is simply that the architect designs his structures in his imagination before he builds them in reality.

Work that is guided by intelligence is the special, unique attribute of humankind. Marx recognized this a century and a half ago. He wrote:

He opposes himself to nature as one of her own forces, setting in motion arms and legs, head and hands, the natural forces of his body in order to appropriate nature's productions in a form adapted to his own wants. By thus acting on the external world and changing it, he at the same time changes his own nature.[5]

The peculiar ability of work to change humankind and for humankind to be influenced and changed by its work has long been recognized. "The hand," said Engles, "is not only the organ of labor, it is also the product of labor."[6] Sir Winston Churchill is said to have said, "We form our buildings, then our buildings form us."

Aristotle termed work simply, "intelligent action," which is perhaps the best definition of all and the one that will be used here.[7] Although work has always been held in higher regard by those who philosophized rather than sweated over it, it has been recognized by philosophers and laborers alike that work transcends mere instinctual activity and defines the basic, essential difference between humankind and insect and animal builders.

We assume that sometime after the beginning, when humankind learned to work and to give it undivided attention, the idea of design, separate from work, came into being. Design defined as a mental project or scheme in which means to an end are projected and a particular purpose is held in mind, is simply the "intelligence" in the "intelligent action" of Aristotle's definition of work. It is this element in work that distinguished humankind's work from the instinctive activities of insects, weaverbirds, and aardvarks.

15

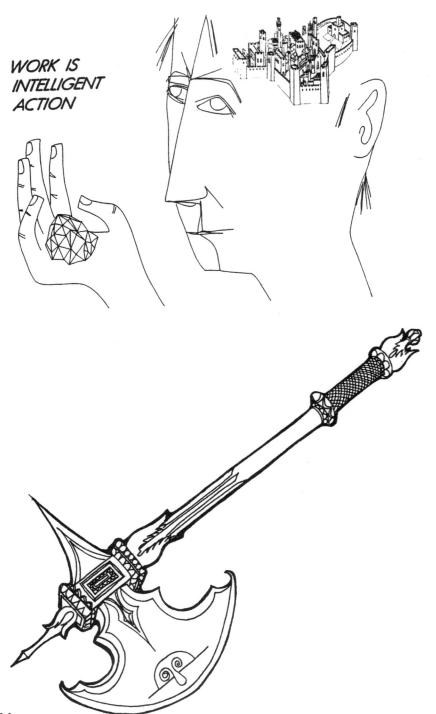

WORK IS INTELLIGENT ACTION

As Marx, Engles, Churchill, and Aristotle seem to agree, the results of our work will shape future generations, as we have been shaped by the work of those who came before us. It seems obvious that our attitude toward work--who benefits, who does not, who is a professional, and who is not--is more significant to our future than many of our religious and political beliefs, philosophies, or even the fate of Mary Hartman.

We find in the history of work that there are two definite categories. One category is work that is devoid of intelligent action, in which people band together to perform tasks for their own benefit. If they do not do this willingly, they must therefore be forced to work by coercion and fear. The second category, work which involves intelligent action, is performed willingly and joyfully without coercion. Our concern is with work that has been divested of intelligent action and the consequences that arise because of it.

When Domenico Fontana erected the obelisk in the piazza in front of Saint Peter's in 1586 a large number of workmen were employed. The work was menial, excruciatingly hard, and very dangerous. Fontana used the death penalty to maintain a proper working attitude.[8] A public executioner stood ready at the erection site. This, to my knowledge, is the first recorded use of industrial psychology.

An evaluation of work in this regard would produce the following ratio: the more intelligent action bestowed on work by individual workmen, the less need there is for coercion. Conversely, the less intelligent action involved in work, the more need there is for management, coordination, design, fear, and headsmen.

The application of this ratio to our own time, as well as to that of Fontana, tells us a good deal about the buildings we build and the society we live in and the position of designers within it. If this is true, and it is difficult to deny, what of work in our society? This is not a subject written about very often. However, Studs Terkel wrote a book entitled Working, in which he summed up the attitudes of the great majority of American working men and women.

This book, being about work, is, by its very nature, about violence to the spirit as well as to the body. It is about ulcers as well as accidents, about shouting matches as well as fistfights, about nervous breakdowns as well as kicking the dog around.

(Courtesy of General Motors Corporation)

$$\frac{\text{intelligence}}{\text{action}} = \frac{\text{design}}{\text{drudgery}}$$

*It is above all or beneath all, about daily humiliations.
To survive the day is triumph enough for the walking
wounded among the great many of us....It is about a search,
too, for daily meaning as well as daily bread, for recognition as well as cash, for astonishment as well as torpor;
in short, for a sort of life rather than a Monday through
Friday sort of dying. Perhaps, immortality too, is part
of the quest. To be remembered was the wish, spoken and
unspoken, of the heroes and heorines of this book.*[9]

This is not a description of people expending intelligent
action in their work, banded together voluntarily to help each other
raise a house or barn. It is, instead, a description of bone-weary
people, peering fearfully over their shoulders at the shadow of the
headsman as they strain at the ropes to raise the obelisk. What if
the buildings we build and shape, shape us, as Churchill claimed
they do? Will the hand that evolves from work under these conditions
regress from fingers and thumb to the claws and talons of bird and
animal builders?

Work in our time, perhaps more than in any other in history,
although the process of division is not new, has been divided and
subdivided into increasingly less comprehensible tasks. Only
managers, superintendents, and designers exercise a limited range
of choice and can comprehend something of the finished product,
gaining whatever satisfaction they can from their narrow view. But
architects become architects because of their love of workmanship.
They have little other reason for doing so. As artists they are
associated with the buffoonery of the fine arts. Their monetary
compensation is often less than that received by a mediocre trades-
man. The one universal characteristic, among a highly diverse
group of men and women who become architects, is their love of the
intelligent action in work. The nature of the kind of intelligent
action the architect can bestow upon the work of building is largely
dependent upon the nature of the work relationship between the
designer and those that carry out his or her designs.

A favorite game of archeologists, architects, and historians
seems to be that of guessing how the pyramids were built. Sand
ramps, walking cranes, chain hoists from hovering interplanetary
spacecraft have all been suggested. However, no matter what the
speculation, there are some obvious facts that cannot be contra-
dicted. Barring help outside this world, the pyramids were built
by human work. Whether Herodotus was correct when he estimated
that it took 400,000 men twenty years, or whether Petri's more
modest estimate of 115,000 is near the truth, we cannot be sure.

17

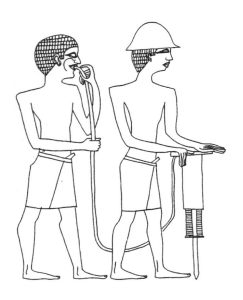

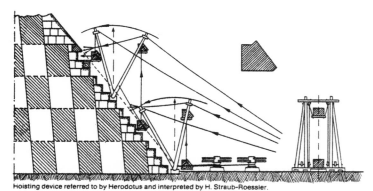

Hoisting device referred to by Herodotus and interpreted by H. Straub-Roessler.

(Pyramid drawings courtesy of Koppers Company, Inc.)

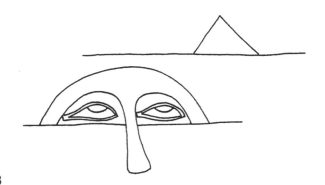

We do know, however, without a doubt, that the historian who wrote "the various labor gangs who worked on the pyramids were imbued with a spirit of pride in their work...," was an idiot. We know further that he never helped to jack-ass tons of stone in the hot sun. An Egyptian Stud's Terkel would have described the work with four-letter hieroglyphs. Yet this nonsensical, historical reading of history is remarkably similar to that made by one of the most revered of modern architects. When Le Corbusier wrote that automobile assembly-line workers took pride in the fact that a car they helped assemble had triumphed in a stock car race, he projected the following fantasy. "The workmen will gather together and tell one another, 'Our Car Did That.' There we have a moral factor that is important."[10] We can be sure that Le Corbusier never spent any time at all "on the line" in an auto factory and that he had absolutely no understanding of the demeaning quality of the industrial work that he proposed as a means to revolutionize the housing industry.

We are told that Imhotep, King Zoser's architect, who, during the third dynasty built the world's first pyramid, was greatly revered. Although Banister Fletcher says he changed his mind five times and Sandestrom claims no less than nine change orders, Imhotep was deified in the twenty-sixth dynasty. We cannot, however, despite the reverence paid this architect, make the mistake of believing that his design involved any more intelligent action on the part of his workers than the work of an auto assembly-line worker. The real truth, if we judge from work, is found in Herodotus, who knew a Terkel situation when he saw one. Speaking of the Great Pyramid at Giza, he wrote, "But Cheopes brought the people to utter misery... he compelled all Egyptians to work for him."

Although we do not know exactly how many slaves it took to put the stones of a pyramid in place, we do know that all Egyptian building projects had a great number of scribes, managers, clerks of the works, field superintendents, subcontractors, sacred alligators, and executioners. Yet, in memory of this horrendous human effort of men, supervisors, and alligators, the name of Cheopes is the only one associated with the Great Pyramid of Giza. Similarly, Ford is the only name on the millions of cars that come off the assembly line at River Rouge.

Such relationships have not always held true. We know something of the conditions under which Roman architects worked from Vitruvius. He wrote his famous Ten Books of Architecture as a public relations gesture to ingratiate himself with the emperor, Ceasar Augustus, in the first century A.D.

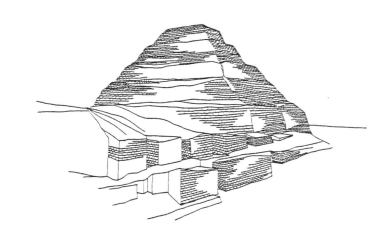

$$\frac{\text{IMHOTEP}}{200{,}000 \text{ fellahin} \times 20 \text{ years}} = \text{PYRAMID}$$

We assume Vitruvius was a run-of-the-mill Roman architect, unusual only in his flare for public relations. Even though the Romans were not particularly selective about whom they chose to deify, we do not expect Vitruvius to be among the pantheon of Roman gods. We can't really identify for sure any of the buildings he designed.

We know something also of the work of the Master Masons of medieval times from fragments of writing here and there. But most of the evidence is in the anonymous craftsmanship of the buildings they helped put into place. Despite this magnificent accomplishment, evidenced by so much intelligent action in wood, metal, and stone, except for a few exceptions among hundreds of cathedrals built, the Master Masons remain anonymous builders.

How did we revert to the mindless work of pyramid builders in the twentieth century? How were the majority of American workers reduced to a level of insect and animal activity?

Seigfried Gideon tells us that industrialists hit upon the happy idea of considering workmen as machine tools, thereby instituting a new and original concept of industrial management.[11] Prior to the discovery that this could be done, workers simply sold their time. Strikes were held against the fourteen- , twelve- , ten-hour days. "Scientific management," as the new idea was termed, forced men into machinelike actions timed by stopwatches. Craftsmanship was eliminated from the work place and became the property of management.

By the first decade of this century, the stopwatch had become outdated and time/motion studies instituted. Frank B. Gilbreth, an American production engineer, fixed lights to workers' bodily extremities and photographed their actions on slow film.[12] Gideon heralded this as an artistic breakthrough. The early cubists were thrilled. Picasso used the technique in his paintings and Duchamp's Nude Descending Staircase was a much heralded artistic outcome of time/motion study.

At this point, it might be well to define an essential difference between craftsmanship and technology. Craftsmanship is that particular ability that workmen develop as their individual attribute. It cannot be taught, but can be learned. Technology is transferable knowledge that has been defined, codified, standardized, and recorded.

19

master mason
free stone cutters
masons
carpenters
smiths
———— = CATHEDRAL
donkeys
oxen

Technology can be contained in books, instruction manuals, and taught in schools. It is transferable, does not depend on any individual, and has little to do with quality. Craftsmanship tends to be eliminated by industrial management and technology substituted in its place.

The architects of the modern movement, like the artists, saw only the possibilities of design in industrialization, and none of them, except for a few eccentrics like Morris and Ruskin, noted the systematic elimination of intelligent action and the accompanying degradation of the great mass of ordinary workers. No Gorki arose among the artists or architects to describe the lower depths of the assembly line. Only Utopian dreams of radiant cities were put forth. This is even the more remarkable because architects are craftsmen. They become architects because of their love of the craft, their love of intelligent action, which they call "design."

By the time Henry Ford perfected the assembly line, about 1913, scientific management was so taken for granted that he did not even mention Frederick Taylor, whom some say was the inventor. By the Second World War, scientific management was advanced enough for the United States to build a Liberty ship a day, just a little faster than the ships were sunk by the German Navy who was building submarines in the same manner.

World War II brought with it a new generation of tools. Some say that these were merely the evolution of the earlier tools of the Industrial Revolution. They were, in fact, entirely new. The tools of the Industrial Revolution extended muscle power; as thinkers they were hulking idiots. But the new tools of World War II and after extended the senses-- television, radar, sonar, the computer. These are design, not muscle, tools. They are used in facilitating intelligent action. The designer, manager, coordinator now face the specter of a repetition of history in the industrialization of intelligent action. This time they become the assembly line workers. The specter of the "creative assembly line" of "stopwatch intuition" of "time study inspiration" appears. Will industrial psychologists open a designer's skull and fix a light to his brain to follow the path of an idea? Can we stop-watch architects and control their motions to produce twenty feet of preliminary sketches per second, and in unison?

The crisis that architects and all designers face today is simply an extension of the crisis of all working people. It is

(Courtesy of General Motors Corporation)

$$\frac{\text{Industrial Designer}}{\text{10,000 workers x 1 second}} = \text{Ford}$$

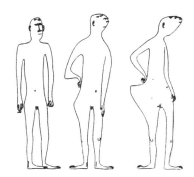

the crisis of their work activity in this world, its meaning, how we form it, and how it forms us. It is the turn now of managerial, design, and supervisory workers to lose their craftsmanship and have technology substituted in its place. It is their turn to become computer assembly-line workers, drafting machine operators, gold fish in "think" tanks.

It does not seem that the intrinsic characteristic of the work itself is significant, but rather, it is the exercise of human intelligence that gives work meaning. The work of selling ribbons can be made significant and the life and death tasks of a laboratory technician boring. People continually devote earnest effort to inconsequential tasks and make life and death decisions frivolously.

The creative satisfaction of the intelligent action of one single designer is paid for in the "...violence to the spirit as well as to the body...ulcers as well as accidents...shouting matches as well as fist fights...nervous breakdowns...daily humiliations..."[13] suffered by the hundreds and thousands of those that carry out the designer's instructions on the assembly line.

The one peculiar, most degrading aspect of work today is the extreme division of labor. Craftsmen have always divided and systematized their work to increase their efficiency. But workers will never willingly labor at one single repetitive work operation continuously unless coerced. In the early nineteenth century women and children mill workers were preferred and constituted the major labor force. In a "Philosophy of Manufacturers" published in 1835, a Mr. Ure wrote, "it is found nearly impossible to convert persons past the age of puberty into useful factory hands, whether they come from agriculture or handcrafts."[14]

The craft skill of the artisan is separated into separate activities and divided among unskilled and semiskilled workmen. They are paid lower rates, perform one task unceasingly, and are as interchangeable as machine parts. The pride of workmanship, which afforded workmen and women a unique identity among their peers is eliminated. As work is simplified and machines become complex, workmen simply mark time until eliminated. Intensified labor division now permeates all branches of work activity. Commercial office work is now standardized. Pay and status advantages over factory work have disappeared. Design offices imitate their industrial clients by separation and by standardizing work tasks.

SAINTE-MARIE-DE-LA-TOURETTE, LE CORBUSIER, ARCHITECT
(From THE NEW CHURCHES OF EUROPE by G. E. Kidder Smith)

"The art advances the artisan recedes."

Draftsmen, specification writers, construction superintendents, computer programmers carry out the specialized tasks formerly performed by the single architect-craftsman. The entire design office may concentrate on only one building type, such as office buildings, hospitals, or stores. The system of work division, no matter where it's practiced, in the factory or office, eliminates general skills and brings into being specialized activities. As these single tasks become more complex, their adherents petition to be awarded professional status. The janitor calls himself the "building superintendent," the air-conditioning mechanic, the "environmental engineer," the interior designer, an "interior architect." The registered nurse seeks liability insurance so that she or he will be considered professional.

As each step of production is isolated and reduced to thoughtless action, workers are systematically deprived of special training and knowledge. The relatively few of whom intelligent decisions are asked are freed from performing labor tasks. At one end of the scale are the professionals whose time is extremely valuable; at the other are interchangeable workmen whose time has almost no value at all. This division is fundamental to industrial management for it exists in greater or lesser degree in all industry and in all nations, regardless of political ideology.

Alexis de Tocqueville, the Studs Terkel of his day, pointed out the inherent dangers almost a century and a half ago.

Can it be believed that the democracy which has overthrown the feudal system and vanquished kings will retreat before tradesmen and capitalists...when a workman is engaged every day upon the same details, the whole commodity is produced with greater ease, speed, and economy...when a workman is increasingly and exclusively engaged in the fabrication of one thing, he ultimately does his work with singular dexterity; but at the same time he loses the general faculty of applying his mind to the direction of the work. Every day he becomes more adroit and less industrious; so that it may be said of him that in proportion as the workman improves, the man is degraded. What can be expected of a man who has spent twenty years of his life in making heads for pins? And to what can that mighty human intelligence which has so often stirred the world be applied in him except it be to investigate the best method of making pin heads?...in proportion as the principle of

22

ONE OF THE FIRST APPLICATIONS OF THE MOVING ASSEMBLY LINE, MAGNETO ASSEMBLY OPERATION AT THE FORD MOTOR COMPANY HIGHLAND PARK PLANT, 1913 (Courtesy of FORD Motor Co.)

HOUSING FOR WORKERS OF A PACKING CRATE FACTORY, DESIGNED BY LE CORBUSIER, PESSAC, FRANCE 1926.

the division of labor is more extensively applied, the workman becomes more weak, more narrow-minded, and more dependent. The art advances, the artisan recedes. [15]

The manifestos and pronouncements of the architects, artists, and designers at the beginning of this century dramatically affirmed the continued and persistent denegration of industrial workmen and ignored the persistent revulsion of the workers for industrialized labor. The German artist Herman Mathesius, who some hail as "the father of the modern movement" in art, wrote in 1914:

The whole area of Werkbund's activities is pressing towards standardization...standardization, to be understood as the result of a beneficial concentration, will alone make possible the development of a universally valid, unfailing good taste. [16]

Le Corbusier understood the work process:

The worker makes one tiny detail, always the same one, during months of work, perhaps during years of work, perhaps for the rest of his life. He only sees his task reach its finality in the finished work at the moment when it is passed, in its bright and shiny purity, into the factory yard to be placed in a delivery van.... [17]

What is the man going to do with his freedom from 6 A.M. till 10 P.M...what becomes of the family under these conditions. The lodging is there you will say to receive and welcome the human animal, and the worker is sufficiently cultivated to know how to make a healthy use of so many hours of liberty. But this is exactly what is not the case; the lodging is hideous, and his mind not sufficiently educated to use all these hours of liberty. We may well say, then architecture or demoralization-- demoralization and revolution. [18]

This is not the utterance of an early nineteenth century industrialist who advocates the hiring of women and children because of their docility, but the polemic of an idealist architect of the twentiety century--a man who understood the degrading conditions of work and described them in detail. Le Corbusier then proposed that houses be designed for industrial workers using the principles of industrial work so repugnant to them. But the master stroke is to threaten the industrialists with the specter of revolution should they not comply.

(Courtesy of Aluminum Company of America)

The modern movement in architecture was not opposed to craftsmanship. It simply considered it too good for common workmen. In the hands of the artist and architect, work and craftsmanship were glorified.

The Bauhaus wants to educate architects, painters, and sculptors of all levels, according to their capabilities, to become competent craftsmen or independent creative artists and to form a working community of leading and future artist-craftsmen. These men, of kindred spirit, will know how to design buildings harmoniously in their entirety, structure, finishing ornamentation and furnishings.[19]

Bauhaus students were expected to assimilate the essence of all craft knowledge and skill during a few short years of academic discipline. They even usurped the work titles of the craftsmen they displaced and were known as apprentices, journeymen, and junior masters in the historic tradition of the honorable trades.

The designers sided with those who reduced labor to degrading work and then, ironically, complained of the lack of public taste and craftsmanship. Designers extoll the potentials of industrialized building and damn the working force incapable of traditional craftsmanship. Designers insist on designing the icons of industrialized, computerized, mechanized, homogenized buildings, but design them to be hand-assembled.

Yet, what kind of workmanship can be expected of men whose bowels and bladders must be controlled and coordinated to urinate and deficate in unison during ten-minute morning and afternoon rest periods, who do not have time to scratch their noses, who must grasp a tool in a certain way and spend hours, days, weeks, and months tightening an identical thirteen bolts on an identical frame until the next year's model increases or decreases the number? There is little in such work to inspire either aesthetic appreciation, political responsibility, or moral principles. Le Corbusier's radiant city is another Pruitt-Igoo housing project inhabited by Studs Terkel's workmen.

When people are forced to perform meaningless tasks they feel that they themselves are meaningless, as Terkel so vividly documented. The workman who makes throwaway products begins to consider himself a throwaway product. What then is the function

...like cleaning the Augean stables

after the horse been stole
Pogo

(Courtesy of General Motors Corporation)

of design? The worker who now owns an automobile earns its price on an assembly line. The designer who owns a condominium is a mechanical draftsman.

It seems that the designers of the modern movement, who intended to change the world through alliance with the industrialists, backed a losing horse. They had no way of knowing when they placed their bets early in this century that the horse they backed was from the Augean stables. The Augean stables were dirty for good reason; the horses were man-eaters.

Today's designers will need some of the strength and all of the guile of a Hercules to aid people in the task of making themselves comfortable in the world. However, there does seem to be one certainty concerning this labor and that is that designers will no more be able to use the techniques they now employ and the attitudes they now hold than could Hercules have industrially managed the cleaning of the Augean stables.

footnotes

1. Konrad Wachsman – Interview with F. Wilson, Los Angeles, 1970.
2. Nikolaus Pevsner – AN OUTLINE OF EUROPEAN ARCHITECTURE, Pelican, N.Y.C., 1943 (p. 175).
3. Howard W. Haggard, M.D. – DEVILS, DRUGS AND DOCTORS, Harper, N.Y.C., 1929 (p. 344).
4. Harry Braverman – LABOR AND MONOPOLY CAPITAL, Monthly Review Press, N.Y.C. and London, 1974 (p. 47).
5. Karl Marx – CAPITAL, Modern Library Edition, N.Y.C., Revised 1906 (p. 198).
6. Karl Marx and Frederich Engles – SELECTED WORKS, Vol. III, Moscow, 1970 (pp. 66, 67).
7. Aristotle – DE PARTIBUS ANIMALLUM, (640A 32).
8. Henry J. Cowan – AN HISTORICAL OUTLINE OF ARCHITECTURAL SCIENCE, Elsevier, N.Y.C., 1966 (p. 17).
9. Studs Terkel – WORKING, Avon, N.Y.C., 1972 (excerpts from introduction).
10. Le Corbusier – TOWARDS A NEW ARCHITECTURE, Praeger, N.Y.C., 1960 (pp. 245-246).
11. Siegfried Giedion – MECHANIZATION TAKES COMMAND, Oxford, 1948; Norton, N.Y.C., 1969 (p. 95).
12. Ibid., (pp. 100-105).
13. Terkel – WORKING, Avon, N.Y.C., Introduction Xiii, 1972.
14. Jurgen Kaczynski – THE RISE OF THE WORKING CLASS, World University Library, McGraw Hill, N.Y.C., 1967 (p. 64).
15. Alexis de Tocqueville – DEMOCRACY IN AMERICA, Vintage Books, N.Y.C., Vol. I (p. 168).
16. Ulrich Conrads, Ed. – PROGRAMS AND MANIFESTOS OF THE 20TH CENTURY, MIT Press, Boston, 1975 (p. 28).
17. Le Corbusier – TOWARDS A NEW ARCHITECTURE, (pp. 245-255).
18. Ibid., (p. 255).
19. Walter Gropius – THE SCOPE OF TOTAL ARCHITECTURE, Collier, N.Y.C., (pp. 44-57).

But they [craftsmen] keep stable the fabric of the world, and their prayer is in the practice of their trade.

SYR. 38:34

DETAILS OF THEME BUILDING EXPO MONTREAL
(Courtesy of Expo Corporation)

Craftsmen

As work projects become larger and more complex, there is a transition from the intelligent action of one craftsman to the coordinated activity of many. Critical dimensions must be determined so that the work of all can be coordinated. Drawing is introduced as a means of planning work.

When a craftsman works alone he makes a series of minor adjustments in a continuous process of fitting parts together. No two of the final finished products are exactly alike. With the introduction of drawings, much larger work is possible and production increases. An artifact that would require several weeks for an individual craftsman to complete is divided into smaller standardized components made simultaneously. Those dimensions that the craftsman would have left undecided in order to adjust to the particular need of a particular client or his own decision as the work progressed are fixed in advance. The division of labor eliminates the possibility of adjustment for unique personal fit and the craftsman's option for intuitive change. Consequently, drawing speeds the work, but results in the production of identical products.

Much of the ability of the individual craftsman to make decisions is removed and given to a new class of workmen who do not work with their hands, but, instead, make decisions concerning the work as a whole. Designing as a separate task comes into being.

The division of work is not a new production system. Archeologists have identified the trademarks of no less than one hundred different vase makers of fifth and sixth century B.C. Attic pottery. Vases were mass-produced as containers for the export of wine and olive oil.

The factory system was adopted in other Greek industries as well. At the end of the fifth century B.C., the father of Demosthenes, the most famous of Attic orators, owned a bedstead workshop employing twenty slaves and an arms factory with thirty-two. A certain Kephalos employed 120 artisans in his shield factory.[1] The division of labor has apparently existed since the beginnings of recorded history and probably even in the flint-flaking and flint-chipping industries before.

MAYAN MODULAR MASONRY AT KABAH, YUCATAN
(Photos by F. Wilson)

MENDING NETS AT FORIO D'ISCHIA (Photo by F. Wilson)

The result of subjecting manufacturing to drawing and design planning as a separate activity is that the designer must visualize a complete entity. The designer manipulates the design and makes changes using ruler and compass on paper, rather than altering the actual material. Successive changes are drawn and redrawn from a single design which the designer has fixed in his mind. Designers are removed from direct contact with the work and must rely on memory, experience, schooling, and imagination to decide what will or will not fit and what can or cannot be made. Once work and intelligence have been separated, it is only a short step to formalization and to cataloguing the intelligence of work into technology.

The change from craftsmanship to draftsmanship is in many ways similar to the present change from design to systems research and the industrialization of the design process with computers. Yet, craftsmanship, design, and technology can remain under the control of the workman as they did during much of industrial manufacturing until the latter part of the nineteenth century.

The period of greatest invention in industry and American building occurred at a time that men and women were adapting their environments to new conditions, building new lives and settling a continent.

Frontier men and women did not rely on traditional answers. They were very short of tradition to begin with. The pioneers were not the elite, the cultured, the nobility, or the upholders of traditions. They were the losers of the established society who sought a new chance on the frontier. They were handymen, laborers, and carpenters, rather than architects; clerks, stock boys, and shopkeepers, rather than merchants. They were grade school teachers and those that were brought up on McGuffey's Readers, rather than professors; barber surgeons and pharmacists, rather than internists and medical researchers. Those that upheld the law were sometimes former outlaws.

To the extent that people were free to react to the physical realities of widely different situations they responded creatively and uniquely, giving truth to the beliefs of Thomas Jefferson and the writings of Horatio Greenough. "I know of no safe depository of the ultimate powers of society, but the people themselves," said Thomas Jefferson. Horatio Greenough wrote in the 1830s:

NOTRE DAME
(Courtesy of French Government Tourist Office)

It is the great multitude for whom all really great things are done and said and suffered....the great multitude desires the best of everything and in the long run is the best judge of it. The monuments, pictures, the statutes of the republic will represent what the people love and wish for, not what they can be made to accept.[2]

Craftsmanship in the United States, because of the nature of its development has been distinctly separate from "art." The working conditions of the American workmen were analogous to those of Gothic builders. Gothic workmen were not concerned with self-conscious concepts of "beauty." Gothic craftsmen did not consider their work "art." Even on the great cathedrals there were only masons and "free" stonecutters. The ordinary mason trued the stones for the structure and the "free" stonecutters carved sculpture. Their chisels were made of the same iron, they cut the same stone, worked side by side, and drank and whored in the same ale houses. Wrote Wilhelm Worringer:

If we speak of beauty in Gothic, it is only because of the poverty of our language, which in this instance certainly conceals a very perceptible poverty in knowledge as well. The so-called beauty of Gothic is a modern misunderstanding. It's true greatness has so little to do with our current conception of art, which of necessity culminates in the idea of 'beauty,' that an acceptance of the word for Gothic values can only cause confusion.[3]

The same misconception often holds true in our interpretation of the work of American builders from the seventeenth to the end of the nineteenth century. Yet if we view art as a creative aspect of work, as did the Gothic builders, and see design as the intelligence of Aristotle's intelligent action, we may call craftsmen artists and artists craftsmen without contradiction.

The particular meaning of the craftsman's creativity must be searched for in writings on aesthetics, for the trade manuals of workmen do not mention this aspect of craftsmanship at all, but simply take it for granted.

CATHEDRAL AND BAPTISTERY, FLORENCE, ITALY
(Courtesy of Italian State Tourist Office)

ITALIAN VILLA (From VICTORIAN PATTERN BOOK CIRCA 1880)

Herbert Read saw mankind's aesthetic sensibility as a permanent, static element of his being. It is the interpretation of this sensibility that varies, Read contended. Although form may be catalogued in intellectual terms, such as measure, balance, rhythm, and harmony, it is essentially intuitive in nature. It is not an intellectual product, but is emotionally defined and directed. Yet similar forms may have a different expressive value for different people and for different periods of civilization. Read concluded:

> *I do not think that we can say that primitive art is a lower form of beauty than Greek art; although it may represent a lower kind of civilization, it may express an equal or even finer instinct for form....I do not know how we are to judge form except by the instinct that creates it.*[4]

Read gives us a definition of form in keeping with the common, rather than the unique, nature of creativity. It coincides with Jefferson's and Greenough's belief in the intelligence of the multitude and the Gothic masons' beliefs about themselves. It is foreign to the concept of the individual genius of a single egocentric designer typified by the "Renaissance man."

The aesthetic sensibility, nowhere more evident than in the works of the mongrel mixture of people that populated the United States, was precisely what has been omitted from the story of American art and architecture according to John Kouwenhoven.

> *Men everywhere and at all times instinctively seek to arrange the elements of their environment in patterns of sounds, shapes, colors, and ideas which are aesthetically satisfying, and it is this instinct which underlies the creation of techniques and forms in which the creative imagination of the artist finds expression.*[5]

Rather than the creativity of the great multitude being the watered down versions of the cultured taste, Kouwenhoven saw the cultured taste leaching its creativity from the robust vitality of the works of ordinary people. Kouwenhoven documented the evolution of the working forms of tools and implements, the inventions and ingenious solutions of men and women engaged in the back-breaking toil of carving a life from the wilderness of a new continent.

GOODELL & WATERS.
Builders of Wood-Working Machinery,

Northwest Corner of 31st and Chestnut Streets,

PHILADELPHIA, PA.

The instinctive desire to create is so well recognized and common an attribute that it is taken for granted by those who possess it. The development of work art forms, which is its most common manifestation, is, therefore, difficult to trace. No one bothers to note the patterns of colors, shapes, sounds, and ideas which are commonly produced. No detailed record is kept until long after the patterns have crystallized and become habitual. They do not become art until designated as such by the cultured tastes and they are recorded and placed in museums. This is usually only long after they have ceased to be of interest to the anonymous people who created them. It is in these unpretentious, crude, vigorous forms that Kouwenhoven found the clearest expression of the vital impulses upon which he predicted the future of modern civilization depended.

The creative relation of the craftsman to his work, like folk art, was seldom recognized. The histories of engineering were usually written by Europeans and were, consequently, slow to recognize the phenomena of unique American creativity, although it was clearly apparent in the comparison of American and European tools and artifacts displayed at the great fair in the Crystal Palace in London, 1851.

The difference between European and American machines and artifacts was due to the difference in the relationship of craftsmen to their work. European machines were rarely designed by craftsmen for their own use. Instead they were designed by professional designers for industrialists who in turn introduced them into their factories to improve production efficiency. The objective of such design was then, as it is now, to make machines that operated as easily and simply as possible. In the United States, on the other hand, machines were designed by craftsmen for their own use or were sold to those who would use them.

American designers had in mind no constants, or rules of proportion. They supplied a shaft here, a pulley there, with bolts and framing to support them. They make their machines like they built their houses and furniture, to suit and fit themselves.[6]

Richards, an English woodworking expert of the mid-nineteenth century, declared that nowhere in the world were there machines for making doors, sash, and wood joinery to equal those of the United States. The tools, it was true, lacked finish and decoration compared to their European equivalents; the movement and the use of the cutting edge was given the first consideration and all else in their design followed this priority.

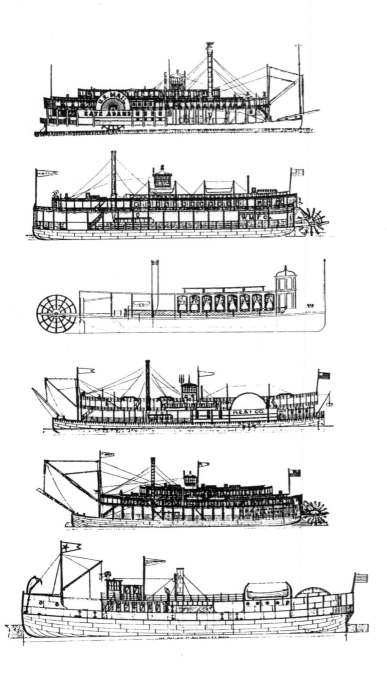

AMERICAN STEAM BOAT DESIGNS
(From the catalog of James Rees and Sons Company of
Pittsburgh, Pa. c. 1850)

Machine design was emperical; machines were ornamented fanci-
fully and painted bright colors. William Sellers of Philadelphia,
whom the English designer, Whitworth, is said to have called "the
greatest mechanical engineer in the world," simply went on the
theory that, "if a machine worked right, it would look right."

John Fritz, one of the developers of the Bessemer steel
process, was typical of the emperical American engineer. It was
reported that his favorite words upon finishing a machine were,
"Now boys, we have got her done. Let's start her up and see why
she doesn't work."[7] This attitude was typical of almost all early
American efforts to pattern the technological environments. The
men who designed and built the clipper ships in the 1840s and 50s
worked in much the same fashion. The essential characteristics
they sought in their designs were economy of line, strength, and
freedom from ornament. Donald McKay's Flying Cloud and Soverign
of the Seas were reported to be not only two of the swiftest sail-
ing ships of their time, but also the most beautiful.

Robert Fulton had failed in his design of steamboats for
the western rivers, but a distinctive riverboat was developed
by a former deckhand, Henry Miller Shreve. Shreve had worked
as a bargeman and later served as captain of the Enterprise,
the first steamer to sail the Mississippi to Louisville. He
knew from working on the rivers what the rivers required. In
1816 Shreve built the Washington. It was different from any
other steam vessel known at that time. Boilers had previously
been set in the ship's hold with upright cylinders. Shreve
mounted them on deck with the cylinders horizontal. He
designed a flat-bottomed hull with a shallow draft similar to
the western river keelboat he knew so well.[8]

Riverboat innovation never ended. No two were alike.
An English engineer, David Stevenson, reported in his Sketch
of the Civil Engineering of North America, that:

> Every American steamboat builder holds opinions of
> his own which are generally founded not on theoretical
> principles, but on deductions drawn from a close
> examination of the practical effects of the different
> arrangements and proportions adopted in the construc-
> tion of different steamboats...the natural consequence
> is, that, even at this day, no two steamboats are alike,
> and few of them have attained the age of six months
> without undergoing material change.[9]

The Wylam Dilly built about 1814 by William Hedley
(From Early American Locomotives by John H. White Jr.
Dover Books)

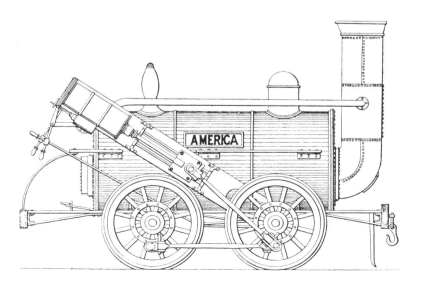

Locomotive by the D and H Canal Company built by
John Stephenson and Company in 1828 (From Early
American Locomotives by John H. White Jr. Dover
Books)

Work and science were connected by craftsman and artisan. The craftsman was the chief repository of scientific production techniques in their existing form. Historical accounts of English designers also emphasize the origins of science in craft techniques.

Said Elton Mays:

Speaking historically, I think it can be asserted that a science has generally come into being as a product of well-developed technical skill in a given area of activity. Someone, some skilled worker, in a reflective moment attempted to make explicit the assumptions that are implicit in the skill itself. Science is rooted deep in skill and can only expand by the experimental and systematic development of an achieved skill. The successful sciences consequently are all of humble origin in the cautious development of lowly skills until the point of logical and experimental expansion is clearly gained.[10]

In a descriptive history of the steam engine in 1824 Robert Stuart Meikleham wrote:

How much of this development [the steam engine] was owing to the science of heat? All available evidence indicates that it was very little. We know not who gave currency to the phrase of the invention [the steam engine] being one of the noblest gifts that science ever made to mankind. The fact is that science, or scientific men, never had anything to do with the matter, indeed there is no machine or mechanism in which the little that theorists have done is more useless. It arose, was improved and perfected by working mechanics, and by them only.[11]

The craftsmen that Meikleham had in mind, who were self-taught engineers and amateur scientists, were hardly uneducated assembly-line workers. They were products of demanding and carefully planned English apprenticeships. We know from the writings of observers of the time that the theoretical knowledge of these craftsmen was astounding.

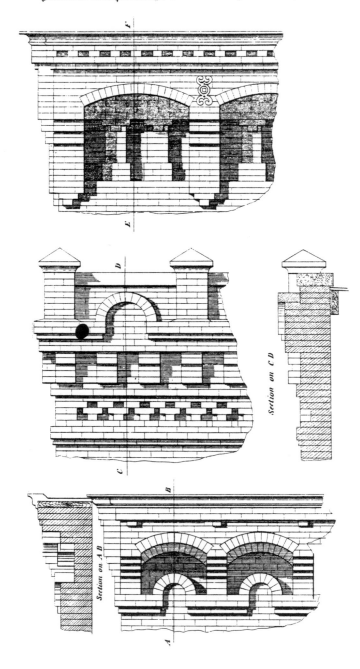

Section on C D

Section on A B

The ordinary millwright was usually quite accomplished in arithmetic, knew something of geometry, and in some instances possessed a competent knowledge of higher mathematics. Many were capable of calculating the velocities of machine parts, the strength of materials, and the power generated by machines. They could draw competently in plan and section, and, as a consequence, were capable of designing both machine and building parts.

These accomplishments were the reflection of the abundant facilities for technical education that the workmen often provided for themselves even in villages such as Manchester during this period. Their schools ranged from dissenters "academica" and learned societies to the invitation of local and visiting lecturers. There were evening schools with classes in mathematics and commerce and a wide circulation of practical manuals, periodicals, and encyclopedias.

The interests of working craftsmen were not confined to their work. They pursued general scientific interests in biology and mathematics, their interests exceeding that of most contemporary college students. Henry Meyhew, an English journalist writing in 1849 to 1850, said the following concerning the English weavers during their "golden age," a period during which they were independent craftsmen:

> *They were formerly, almost the only botanists in the metropolis, and their love of flowers to this day is a strongly marked characteristic of the class. Some years back, we are told, they passed their leisure hours, and generally the whole family dined on Sundays, at the little gardens in the environs of London, now mostly built upon. Not very long ago there was an entomological society, and they were among the most diligent entomologists in the kingdom. This taste, though far less general than formerly, still continues to be a type of the class. There was at one time a floricultural society, an historical society, and a mathematical society, all maintained by the operative silk-weavers; and the celebrated Dolland, the inventor of the archromatic telescope, was a weaver; so too were Simpson and Edwards, the mathematicians, before they were taken from the loom into the employ of government, to teach mathematics to the cadets at Woolwich and Chatham.*[12]

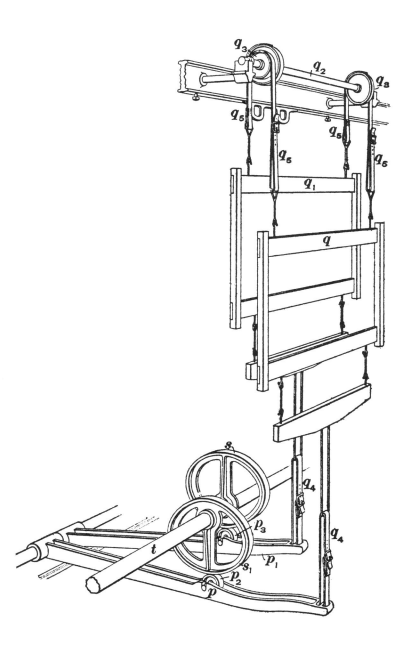

THE CAM LOOM DOMINATED THE AMERICAN WOOLEN INDUSTRY DURING
THE FIRST HALF OF THE NINETEENTH CENTURY.
(Courtesy of Merrimack Valley Textile Museum)

The rise and dominance of the English weaving industry, according to Gideon, occurred precisely because it was the work of commoners. Silk was a luxury textile for a luxury class. The English experimented with cotton from the beginning and built their machines with cotton in mind. Cotton was a rough textile developed by a rough class under rough circumstances through mechanization to mass production.

The inventors were neither nobles nor learned men. Their experiments were not published in the academies and the knowledge of their beginnings must be pieced together from fragments of information. They received no help from their government. The mechanization of production began in the north of England in Lancashire, which was far from the ruling classes and the High Church of England. It began in lonely spots like Manchester, which did not attain corporate status before the nineteenth century and was not bound by guild restrictions. Towns where manufacturers flourished were seldom corporate bodies. Commerce required encouragement instead of privilege. Those who first introduced cotton manufacturing into Lancashire were Protestant refugees, who probably found very little encouragement for themselves and their industries among the corporate towns of England.

John Wyatt, who stretched the yarn between pairs of revolving cylinders instead of by hand, and set up the first small mill in a Birmingham warehouse in 1741, landed in debtors' prison. James Hargreaves, inventor of the "spinning jenny" in the 1750s, was a poor weaver; and Richard Arkwright (1732 to 1792), the first successful cotton spinner, who turned to advantage ideas upon which other men had foundered, was by trade a barber. It was not before 1767 that he turned from his normal calling, which consisted in buying up dull hair and by some process making it usable. In 1780 twenty factories were under his control, and at his death he left his son a large fortune.

The industrial arts were developed by craftsmen. The appearance of the modern engineer is a new social phenomenon. Today's engineer is not the lineal descendant of the old military engineer, but of the millwright and the metalworker of the days of craftsmanship. Those familiar with the history of technology will recognize the importance of the names of Bramah (1748 to 1812), Maudsley (1771 to 1831), Muir (1806 to 1888), Whitworth (1803 to 1887), and the great George Stephenson (1781 to 1881).

(Courtesy of General Motors Corporation)

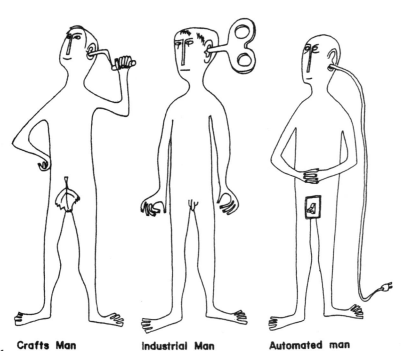

Crafts Man   **Industrial Man**   **Automated man**

To this list can be added the name of James Watt, whose trade was that of mathematical-instrument maker, and Samuel Crompton, who was a spinner from the age of fourteen and continued, in the absence of patent protection, to earn his living as a spinner even after his spinning mule was in widespread use throughout the weaving industry. There were many others, which can be judged by the fact that it was illegal for a British mechanic to accept work abroad up to 1824. The craftsman was the repository of the technical knowledge of the production process and as such was a national resource. Such a restriction is inconceivable today.

Despite the flood of mechanical inventions in recent times, a comparable list cannot be compiled for this century. A study of occupational characteristics of a random sample of persons granted patents in the United States in 1953, conducted by Braverman, showed that about sixty percent were engineers, chemists, metallurgists, and directors of research and development. Almost no production workers were listed.[13]

In a little less than a century the inventiveness, drive for self-improvement, curiosity, and love of work has been transferred from anonymous laborers and craftsmen to men and women holding professional status, who call themselves designers, managers, and research developers.

The reason may be found in the straightforward statement of objectives put forth by Frederick Taylor, who almost single-handedly changed the relation of workmen to their work.[14] Taylor said that the objective of scientific management was simply the control of the intelligence of the action of work. Taylor took a direct route to his objective. He realized that even though management consisted of foremen and superintendents, who themselves were once skilled workers at their trades, it was the workmen themselves who possessed the mass of traditional knowledge of production. The foreman and superintendents knew, perhaps better than any others, that their knowledge and skill fell far short of the combined ability, dexterity, and knowledge of the workmen over which they held jurisdiction.

The most experienced managers placed before their workmen the problem of doing the work in the best and most economical way. The managers recognized their task as that of inducing each workman to use his best endeavors and to work their hardest to exercise the best of their knowledge, skill, and ingenuity.

EARLY GENERAL MOTORS MANUFACTURING PLANT CIRCA 1908
(Courtesy of General Motors Corporation)

CONTEMPORARY GENERAL MOTORS ASSEMBLY LINE
(Courtesy of General Motors Corporation)

In short, it was the workers' initiative that yielded the largest possible return to their employers. Taylor saw this as a danger to management control. Under these conditions the shops were controlled by the workmen. It was therefore impossible for management to set work and production schedules. The first and essential principle that Taylor advocated was that management gather to itself all of the traditional knowledge possessed by the workmen. It was classified, tabulated, and reduced to rules, laws, and formulas. The intelligence of work was removed from the shop and centered in management. This is the key to "scientific management," which is not the management of science, but simply the management of the work process through control of all decisions.

It is possible in human labor, as the success of industrial management has proven, to divorce conception from execution entirely. The price paid for this efficiency in manufacturing is to reduce the work process to that of animal labor. The standards by which workmanship are judged are altered, and the meaning of "skill" itself is degraded.

The control concept adopted requires that every production activity have a parallel in management. Each activity must be devised, precalculated, tested, laid out, assigned, ordered, checked, inspected, and recorded from beginning, during, and upon completion. The result is that the process of production is replicated in paper form before, as, and after it takes place in physical form. Just as labor in human beings requires that the labor process take place in the brain of the worker, as well as in the worker's physical activity, so now the image of the process is removed from production to a separate location and a separate group which controls the process itself.

The uniqueness of this development lies not as much in the separation of hand and brain, conception and execution, but in the rigor with which they are divided and increasingly subdivided further away from each other. Conception is concentrated as much as possible in increasingly limited groups within management. As work becomes, as Studs Terkel documented, "an act of aggression against the workmen themselves," hand and brain are not merely separated, but divided and hostile. Frederick Taylor demanded, as an absolute necessity of scientific management, the dictation to the worker of the precise manner in which work was to be performed. It has always been tacitly agreed by worker and management that the employer has the right to direct labor and owns the products of labor.

EARLY TWENTIETH CENTURY MACHINE CRAFTSMEN

HAND FROM GUERNICA
(Drawing after
Picasso)

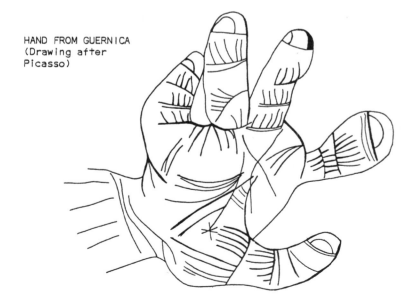

Before the full exploitation of the possibilities in industrial management had been realized, direction had been limited to the assignment of tasks with little direct interference with the method of performing them. Industrial management brought into being a new means for management to achieve control of the actual mode of performance of every labor activity from the simplest to the most complex. As a result, a far greater revolution in the process of work took place than any that had gone before.

Before and during the earliest days of the Industrial Revolution, the skilled craftsman or craft itself was the basic work unit, the elementary cell of the labor process. Innovation, invention, and the beginnings of science or discoveries that science was later to claim and develop began at this point. Each worker possessed the accumulated knowledge of materials and processes by which production was accomplished. It was sifted and perfected through his and her unique experiences and emerged as the act of intelligent action which Aristotle called "work." Anonymous inventions, innovation, and leaps of creative inspiration occurred at the level of craftsmanship.

With the elimination of craft skills and reduction of the workmen to anonymous producers, management now depends upon designers, managers, and superintendents over whom it exercises control. Professional designers emerged when labor had been reduced to unthinking, anonymous producers.

The leaders of the "modern movement" in architecture--Gropius, Mies, Le Corbusier--at this moment in history chose to produce a new aesthetic that glorified this managerial accomplishment. Gropius proposed an elite group of designers who would embody the attributes of super-craftsmen in all trades, like the Renaissance artists who could paint, sculpt, and design fortifications. In the industrial world this meant the design of machine products from ashtrays to skyscrapers or, as Gropius termed the activity, "total design." Of the objectives of the Bauhaus program Gropius said:

The ultimate aim of any creative activity is building ...architects, sculptors, painters, we all must become craftsmen again...no essential difference exists between the artist and the craftsman, the artist is a craftsman of heightened awareness...but the basis of craftsmanship is indispensable to all artists. It is the prime source of all creative work.[15]

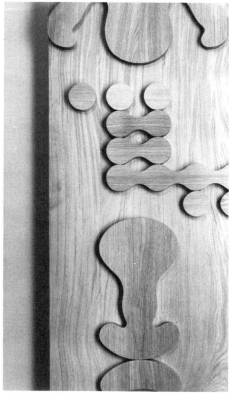

SUMMER METOPE BY JEAN ARP 1946
(Courtesy of The Museum of Modern Art)

AUTOMATIC NAILER
(Courtesy of SENCO Products, Inc.)

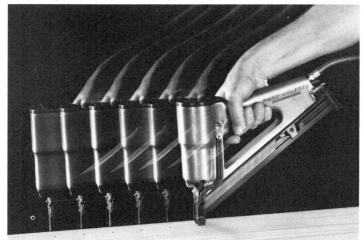

Gropius proposed to train designers from the nursery to maturity. It was these super-designers, the artists and architects, who were to assume all the characteristics of craftsmanship that had been eliminated from the working days and nights of the great multitude of working people. The creativity of the craftsman, and the collective design sensibility of weavers, pattern-making cabinet-makers, sailors, engineers, bargemen, steam fitters and those who had invented riverboats, perfected the steam engines, built bridges, trestles, and devised new building types, all of which had been eliminated from the industrial process by industrial management, were to be replaced in the single person of the artist-craftsman.

The workman's lifetime of work experience, which made him a craftsman and unique among his fellows, was to be assimilated by the Bauhaus student in two or three terms of shop work. Johannes Itten, who was asked to the Bauhaus to form the nucleus of the first course in 1919 to 20 wrote:

To make the student's choice of career easier...exercises with materials and textures were a valuable aid ....unfortunately at the time the basic course did not have a workshop where all the basic skills such as planning, filing, sawing, bending, gluing, and soldering could be practiced.[16]

The artists, architects, and designers of the modern movement proposed "creative management," where Frederick Taylor had so successfully implemented "scientific management." The possiblities were exhilirating for the new craftsmen.

Said Le Corbusier:

Cars, cars, speed, speed! One is carried away, seized by enthusiasm, by joy, not by enthusiasm at seeing the shiny bodywork glistening in the light of the headlamps. But enthusiasm over the joy of power. The frank, ingenious enjoyment of being at the center of power, of energy. We share the power. We are part of this society, confident that it will find the magnificent expression of its energy. We believe in it....the machine gives our dreams their audacity: they can be realized.[17]

MASS PRODUCED VILLA Le Corbusier

COTROHAN HOUSE 1921 Le Corbusier

(Drawings after designs by Le Corbusier)

In contrast to Le Corbusier's dream is Terkel's reality:

I start the automobile, the first welds. From there it goes to another line, where the floor's put on, the roof, the trunk hook, the doors; then it's put on a frame. There are hundreds of lines.

The welding gun's got a square handle, with a button on the top for high voltage and a button on the bottom for low. The first is to clamp the metal together. The second is to fuse it.

The gun hangs from a ceiling, over tails that ride on a tract. It travels in a circle, oblong, like an egg. You stand on a cement platform, maybe six inches from the ground....

I don't understand how come more guys don't flip. Because you're nothing more than a machine when you hit this type of thing. They give better care to that machine than they will to you. They'll have more respect, give more attention to that machine. And you know this. Somehow you get the feeling that the machine is better than you are. [Laugh]

You really begin to wonder. What price do they put on me?...

Phil Stallings, spot welder.[18]

Until near the end of the last century American craftsmen had been the primary builders, designers, inventors, innovators, and managers of their work as had been the English craftsmen a century before. But a drastic change occurred coinciding with Frederick Taylor's implementation of scientific management and its adoption through the last years of the nineteenth century and the first decades of the twentieth.

The professional designers that today profess to possess the esoteric knowledge and unique skill that will assure the quality of the built environment were spawned at precisely the moment that the responsibility and intelligence of work had been wrenched from the craftsmen.

AUTOMOBILE BODY FINISHING IN 1918
FINAL ASSEMBLY CHECK OF CHEVROLETS, FLINT, MICHIGAN 1918
(Photos courtesy of General Motors Corporation)

footnotes

1. Gordon Childs — WHAT HAPPENED IN HISTORY, Pelican, Baltimore, 1942 (pp. 208-209).
2. Horatio Greenough — FORM AND FUNCTION, University of California Press, Berkeley, Calif., 1962 (pp. 79-80).
3. Wilhelm Worringer — FORM IN BOTHIC, Schocken, 1964 (Putnam 1927) London (p. 11).
4. Herbert Read — THE MEANING OF ART, Pelican, Baltimore, 1949 (p. 21).
5. John Kouwenhoven — THE ARTS IN MODERN AMERICAN CIVILIZATION, Norton Library, Baltimore, 1967 (p. 3).
6. Ibid., (p. 3).
7. Ibid., (p. 27).
8. Ibid., (p. 27).
9. Ibid., (p. 28).
10. Harry Braverman — LABOR AND MONOPOLY CAPITAL, Monthly Review Press, N.Y.C., 1967 (p. 134).
11. Ibid., (p. 158).
12. Eileen Yeo and E. P. Thompson, Eds. — THE UNKNOWN MEYHEW, Schocken Books, N.Y.C. (pp. 105-106).
13. Harry Braverman — LABOR AND MONOPOLY CAPITAL, Monthly Review Press, N.Y.C. (p. 132).
14. Ibid., (p. 102).
15. Walter Gropius — SCOPE OF TOTAL ARCHITECTURE, Collier Books, N.Y.C., 1962 (p. 22).
16. Johannes Itten — DESIGN AND FORM, The Basic Course At The Bauhaus and Later, Van Nostrand Reinhold, N.Y.C., (p. 8).
17. Ulrich Conrads — PROGRAMS AND MANIFESTOES, 20th Century Architecture, MIT Press, Cambridge.
18. Studs Terkel — WORKING, Avon, N.Y.C., 1972 (p. 227).

TRIUMPH OF THE EGG, I. BY JOHN FLANNAGAN (1937)
(From the Photo Collection of The Museum of Modern Art, New York)

THE TRIUMPH OF THE EGG

AND THE EGG-BEATER

GREEK-ATTIC VASE, EARLY V CENTURY B.C.
(Courtesy of The Metropolitan Museum of Art, Fletcher Fund, 1956)

Technology

"Technical" and "technology" seem to have been different kinds of words to the ancient Greeks. They used "technical" to refer to art and skillfulness, and "technology" for the systematic treatment of an art. These definitions mix art, skillfulness, and systematic treatment in a way foreign to the extreme division between our worlds of art and work. To us a work of art may or may not be skillful, but it is never in any way related to systematic treatment. Systematic work, as we know it, is relegated to the assembly line.

In the working world of the ancient Greeks, there apparently was no distinction made between art, skillfulness, and the systematic treatment of work. It is very difficult for us today to think of classic Greek vases as technical products even though they were commonly manufactured on pottery assembly lines.

In our industrial society the distinction is clear. Craftsmanship is the result of a relationship between the worker and the material worked. It is not a systematic treatment, but a practical task performed artistically. Any workman can perform a task either systematically or artistically, but never the two together.

The machinist who fixes and operates machines may be a machine craftsman, but the product of the machine is not a craft product, it is a by-product of machine craftsmanship. Craftsmanship is found only in work performed with art and skillfulness which machines cannot do.

We have come to view technology as distinct from craftsmanship and as that body of knowledge about performing work systematically that can be taught, recorded, and passed on from one workman to the other. No amount of management will turn a poor workman into one who works with art and skillfulness. Only the worker himself can do so.

Eric Hoffer poignantly described the contradiction between the workman's skill and the tasks he is forced to perform. Hoffer prided himself on his skill as a sorter. This is the work of separating and assembling the tons of cargo from the ship's hold to be dispatched to its final destination. Hoffer made a game and prided himself on his skill in distinguishing the characteristics of the individual cartons.

STONEHENGE
(Courtesy of CBS News Service)

He developed his ability to sense a similarity in the way crates were packaged and glued, their shape, or the way the label was applied. In this way he managed to derive pleasure and satisfaction from long hours of back-breaking work. "And all I was afraid [of] was the one moment [when] one of these cartons will bust open and will show me the crap they contained, and all my ingenuity and all my energies went on sorting this sort of crap!"

Machine industrialization has obscured the worth of things made which was formerly measured in terms of the human energy and skill required to fashion them. The change occurred some time during the Industrial Revolution as humankind put its mind to inventing machines to ease its back.

From what we know of prehistory, humankind's relation to its work was a simple, hard, grim, cruel life-and-death struggle. Survival depended upon the artifacts that humans could produce. Stored food was insurance against starvation, shelter preserved vital body heat in extremes of temperature, and weapons protected against predators and other humans. Survival was a nip and tuck proposition with humankind's toolmaking and tool-using ability affording a slight edge over those other creatures who contested with them for survival.

Human activity had a no-nonsense value. Fire sustained life and life's worth was measured by the energy that it took to cut and gather firewood. The value of a wooden shelter or crude stone enclosure lay in the sweat and fatigue it required to build and in its effectiveness in preserving human life.

The worth of human life throughout most of history was measured simply in the work a human could do. The physically defective newborn child was strangled or left on the hillside to die. The old who no longer had the vitality to produce as much food as they ate, gather fuel for the warmth they required, or who took up more space than they could build went off and died. The value of artifacts was measured in human skill and human energy. The reward of work was survival.

The muscle machines of industrialization obscured the simple equation of human skill and energy expended to life-sustaining work. The craftsman's abilities were applied to making machines more efficient and complex. Human energy is difficult to measure against machine power. A strong man or woman can compare his or her strength to a horse because both are derived from muscles.

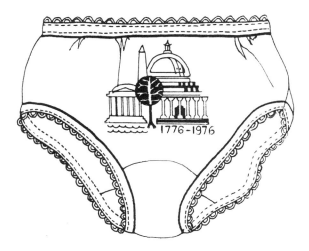

#0976 Woodies own Bicentennial
bikini in white nylon with red/white/
blue emblem, sizes 5-7.
Daywear, all stores.

1976 ADVERTISEMENT BY WOODWARD AND LOTHROP DEPARTMENT
STORE APPEARING IN THE WASHINGTON D.C. POST

STONEHENGE
(Courtesy of CBS News Service)

A stream's current or a wind's force can be felt and the gears that transform water and wind power to useful work are comprehensible devices. But as machines progressed from stream to steam, combustion engines, and electric power, goods are produced without apparent sweat or fatigue. When the power of two hundred horses can be contained underneath an automobile hood and activated by the pressure of a child's foot on a lever, then human strength and hand dexterity are no longer comprehensible units of measure.

Artifacts no longer appear essential to sustain human life; many have become frivolous gadgets. It is only in times of technical malfunction, such as power failures, when we are thrown back upon our muscle resources, and have to climb the stairs of skyscrapers that we realize the existence of the energy to life-sustaining ratio.

The shape of our indifferent buildings affords us no clues as to the value of work. Architects tend to call the human energy dimension "human scale," although it is seldom defined in terms of work, but in terms of size. The basis of human scale is the relationship between hands and human strength in the work we do. Size is important, but incidental. Those elements of the built environment that indicate comprehensible units of human energy always possess human scale. A brick wall is comprehensible because of the relation of a brick's size to the human hand. The way the bricks are laid is an indication of skill. In contrast it is almost impossible to tell whether a space rocket at Cape Kennedy is the real thing or a child's toy, unless a tree, building, or human being is close enough to furnish contrast. The skillfulness of the space engineer is obscured by the technical accomplishment of the machines that made the rocket.

The changing shape of our physical world challenges our atavistic memories of form and space. As forms dictated by engineering increasingly dominate our urban world we are disoriented. Since childhood we have been aware that the buildings that surround and protect us from the elements hold in suspension overwhelming man-crushing weights of timber, stone, steel, and concrete. We are subconsciously aware of this precarious equilibrium that prevents them from tumbling down upon our heads. The logic of force and counterforce has been verified countless times beginning with our first tottering infant steps as we struggle to hold ourselves upright upon our wobbly ankles.

SCALe

We have assured ourselves that gravity pulling toward the center of the earth is the force that holds together the shells of man-made space. We have, over time, developed a sense of the rightness of size for structural members and the logical geometry of building.

This assurance is challenged by the silhouettes, sections, facades, and profiles of modern structures that do not resemble the forms stored in our memories of things that can be made with human hands. They lack the reassuring, familiar geometry and points of human reference of human scale.

Almost anyone can design a building that has spans of thirty or forty feet between its walls and is a few stories high. Little engineering skill is required and the parts can be found in catalogues. But a building span of three hundred or four hundred feet and several hundred feet high demands that the structural form follow the logic dictated by the control of physical forces. The engineering and industrial process and the mobilization of industrial labor to build such a structure is extremely complex. These factors dictate the form of the building. The mark of human hands which establishes what architects term "human scale" is no more apparent in the finished product than it is on the surface of a lunar rocket.

But largeness is not the only perceptual cause of disorientation. Technical knowledge and engineering skill is directed toward the cheapening of all products. Where human life is preserved by human skill and energy, the physical quality of human artifacts, their potential for use over time is a measure of the potential for human survival. Primitive man did not hunt mammoths with plastic spears and New England houses of the seventeenth century did not use plasterboard to keep out the freezing winter winds. Paper dresses, plastic cups, Kleenex, and office temporaries are the products of industrial technology and industrial thinking. Cheap products throughout most of human history indicated disposable people.

The governing force that motivates industrial manufacture is in our time a grand imperative that dictates the turning of inventive skills toward cheapening every product. The combined skill and experience of our best technical minds is devoted to the reduction of the labor and material cost of every building artifact.

SizE is No oBJEct

Samuel Lefrak, a leading housing entrepreneur, expressed his sentiment forthrightly in an interview with the business magazine Forbes.

The government will have to reduce some of the national standards, permit us to use less costly materials, the unions will have to permit a more realistic approach... take out all those restrictive covenants and these high requirements under the zoning laws....[1]

Building is not unique in this respect. The cheapness imperative dominates design and manufacture in all areas. The plastic drinking glass that took the place of the paper cup is cheaper, but too expensive to throw away. We drink from neither disposable nor pleasing containers. The paperback book has increased in price and is now too expensive to discard. Our libraries are full of small-print, cheaply papered, hard-to-read, unpleasant-to-hold books. The ballpoint pen, the plastic dish, the miracle-fiber dress have become part of our semipermanent possessions. We write with, eat from, and wear artifacts that are too expensive to throw away and too cheap to treasure. Yet the obligation to continually cheapen all artifacts is accepted without question by engineers, designers, builders, and architects. Wrote Harry Braverman in his study of labor and monopoly capital:

The equipment is made to be operated; operating costs involve, apart from the cost of the machine itself, the hourly cost of labor, and this is part of the calculation involved in machine design. The design which will enable the operation to be broken down among cheaper operations is the design which is sought by management and engineers who have so internalized this value that it appears to them the force of natural law of scientific necessity.[2]

This does not appear strange to anyone familiar with the development of manufacturing throughout the nineteenth century. "The monogram of our national initials, which is the symbol of our monetary unit, the dollar, is almost as frequently conjoined to the figures of an engineer's calculations as are the symbols indicating feet, minutes, pounds, or gallons," noted Henry R. Towne, a pioneer industrialist and shop manager in a paper read to the American Society of Mechanical Engineers in 1889. "The dollar," he said on a later occasion, "is the final term in almost every equation which arises in the practice of engineering..."

(Photos courtesy of General Motors Corporation)

In the words of a chemist in more recent times, "I'm no longer really interested in problems that don't involve economic considerations. I've come to see economics as another variable to be dealt with in studying a reaction—there's pressure, there's temperature, and there's the dollar."[3]

Cheapening products is not an innocent pastime, although it is a minor infringement upon the relationship between buyer and seller when compared to the lethal effects of product hazards. Industrial design has moved from sharp dealings to what would appear, judging by the casualty lists, an active war upon the users of its products.

The "Final Report of the National Commission on Product Safety" presented to the Congress of the United States in 1970, was the most comprehensive account ever compiled of the perils incurred in this technological civilization.[4] The account documents a devastating record of human injury and suffering.

In the forward to the report the chairman of the committee, Arnold B. Elkind, New York City attorney, stated:

> *When it authorized the Commission, Congress recognized that modern technology poses a threat to the physical security of the consumers. We find the threat to be bona fide and menacing. Moreover, we believe that without effective government intervention the abundance and variety of unreasonable hazards associated with consumer products cannot be reduced to a level befitting a just and civilized society....Perhaps a case can be made for the acceptability of willful personal risk taken by an occasional well-informed consumer, but there is no justification for exposing an entire populace to risks of injury or death which are not necessary and which are not apparent to all. Such hazards must be controlled and limited not at the option of the producer, but as a matter of right to the consumer. Many hazards described in this report are unnecessary and can be eliminated without substantially affecting the price to the consumer. Unfortunately, in the absence of external compulsion it is predictable that there will continue to be an indecent time lag between exposure to a hazard and its elimination.*

Driverless Car Backs Over Owner, Circles as She Dies

By John Harwood
Special to The Washington Post

SEMINOLE, Fla.—Horrified onlookers stood by helplessly yesterday as a runaway automobile backed over its elderly owner, backed over her again, and then circled next to the dying woman for more than 15 minutes.

The runaway 1977 Ford Thunderbird apparently has the type of transmission which the National Highway Traffic Safety

Administration (NHTSA) has warned can slip from park to reverse without warning.

Sixty-seven-year-old Amy Selle was barely alive when paramedics arrived at the accident scene. They found 30 to 40 people gaping ghoulishly at the driverless car as it backed round and round a few feet from Selle. The woman died minutes later.

The car was traveling so fast—15 to 25 miles per hour—that it took fire depart-

ment officials 15 minutes of repeated efforts to stop it.

NHTSA recently warned owners of 1971 to '78 Ford passenger cars that C6 and FMX transmissions may slip from park to reverse. After checking the Florida car's identification number, the Ford Motor Co. said the car apparently has either a C6 or FMX transmission. The NHTSA has received reports of 23 deaths, 259 injuries and 777 accidents allegedly caused by the defects, a spokesman said.

Highway patrol spokesmen said they could not determine whether the gear had slipped from park to reverse.

Told about the accident, NHTSA spokesman Irving Chor said "that's the typical report of a transmission that slipped."

Fire department officials said Selle had stopped by the roadside to pick up a friend. She got out of the car, apparently thinking the gear was in park but when she got out the car moved backwards. She lunged

inside and grabbed at the steering wheel.

But the open door knocked her down into the path of her car, which had pivoted when she turned the wheel.

Paramedics said the car apparently struck Selle twice, fracturing her skull. Then it circled, neatly clipping the corners of an entire intersection.

Fire officials finally stopped the car when one man leaped inside as another held the door open.

NATIONAL COMMISSION ON PRODUCT SAFETY

FINAL REPORT
PRESENTED TO THE PRESIDENT AND CONGRESS
JUNE, 1970

Bicycles

- UPPER TRUNK 4%
- LOWER TRUNK 4%
- WHOLE BODY 1%
- EYE 1%
- UNKNOWN 1%
- HAND 1%
- FACE 23%
- FOOT 1%
- LEG OR ANKLE 21%
- HEAD 14%
- ARM OR WRIST 15%

BODY PART INJURED

SAVE $20

Not intended for stunting or off-road use

**Boys' 20-in.
Deluxe MX-Style Bike**

The annual number of injuries estimated by the National Center for Health Statistics of the Department of Health, Education, and Welfare and the National Safety Council, in and around the American home, indicate that 30,000 people are killed, 110,000 permanently disabled, 585,000 hospitalized, and more than 20 million injured seriously enough to require medical treatment or to be disabled for a day or more. The estimated injuries from consumer products was 14,960,000. Among the most horrifying of these injuries were those caused by recreational equipment. These accounted for eight million injuries--over half the total. Fun and games in America is a lethal pastime. Swings, seesaws, and slides accounted for three-quarters of a million injuries; bicycles, a million.

The elimination of craftsmanship did away with personal responsibility at the point of production. The liability for product safety was passed along to the manager and the designer. The latter assumed it a professional responsibility. For example, architects are licensed for the protection of public health, safety, and welfare. Incidentally, the licenses are issued by the same governmental agency, HEW, that issued the accident figures quoted here.

What is there in the history of design and work relationships that forced the mutation in man-made articles from life-sustaining artifacts, to indifferent products; to lethal objects used at the buyer's risk? Craftsmen accepted personal responsibility for the things they made as part of the pride of work. Technology, on the other hand, is neutral, neither inherently responsible nor irresponsible. Consumers are killed and maimed indifferently without malice or passion.

Karl Marx claimed that social relations, like linen, flax, steel, and buildings, are a product of human work. Therefore, he concluded that social relations are bound to the means of production.

The serf was bound to the noble by the hand mill. The industrial proletariat was bound to the industrialist by the steam engine. We are bound to whomever we are bound in some conglomerate office by electronic devices. The hand mill was accompanied by folk art and craftsmanship. The steam engine gave birth to the industrial production and industrial designer. Electronic devices gave us automation and the programmer. But these relationships are not static. No system is unchanging. Each mutates within itself the seeds of its own obsolescence.

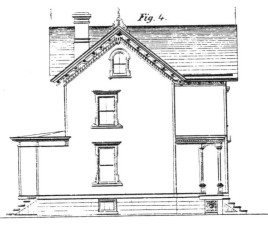

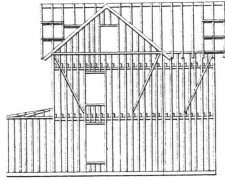

BALOON FRAMED VICTORIAN HOUSE

LOCOMOTIVE BUILT BY THE UNION IRON WORKS
SAN FRANCISCO 1867

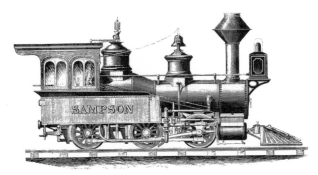

A century and a half ago the simple wire nail and the milling of lumber to 2-inch thicknesses totally altered the concepts of American house building. The hiring of skilled joiners to fit heavy timbers together and the village work force that had formerly gathered to erect heavy timber buildings were no longer necessary. The nail made each man or woman a carpenter. A family alone could build and erect their houses on the great isolated spaces of the West. This small, seemingly insignificant technical change was the basis of that unique, typically American building form, the balloon-frame house. In the short span of half a century balloon-frame houses covered the West and housed a nation in cheap, flimsy houses. They formed the basis of a prefabricated-housing industry far more successful than any we have today and provided houses that burned very satisfactorily in the great Chicago fire.

The manufacturers of the wire nail, the mill owners who cut their logs into scantlings, or the carpenters who devised the framing system were unaware of the fact that they were revolutionizing the house-building techniques of a nation. It is not the extent of knowledge itself or skill that eventually proves effective, but rather a combination of events and purposeful application that produces change. The priests of Yucatan and Guatemala had a firmer grasp of mathematical science than the conquistadores. Numbers were sacred to the Maya. They used them as symbols for the days of the month, to foretell the seasons, to predict eclipses, to plan agricultural cycles, and in other functions unknown to us. In the clash of the two cultures the simple calculation of the trajectory of an iron cannon ball proved of more lasting significance than the calculation of the orbit of the moon or the first day of creation.

The growth and evolution of the productive forces that effect such change occur within the bounds of changing social systems. The balloon-frame house could not have proven such an overwhelming success without free land, railroads, and a jack-of-all-trades building spirit.

The technology of the steam engine helped develop industrial capitalism. Industrial design then evolved as an aspect of industrial technology. Our ideas of design and what designers do are tied to work technology. The industrial designer is as much a result of the steam engine as is the mass production of products on an assembly line.

If industrial products are designed through intent or indifference to be humanly destructive, as documented by the President's

F-15 JETS AND MIDDLE AGES BUILDING COMPLEX
(Courtesy of U.S. Air Force)

Commission on Product Safety, then social relations and productive means must have turned cannibalistic. The craftsman was occasionally responsible for personal injury. The industrial designer gave us industrial accidents, untrustworthy machines, household accidents, and those tragic occurrences documented in the presidential report. But the programmer who works on a much more vast scale can give us nuclear war with the push of a button. It might, therefore, be useful to look closely at the nature of the design and engineering relationships that are developing today in the wake of the industrial designer.

Until recently, during the period of industrialization and before, structural engineers designed intuitively. The Romans built stone arches using every type of stone, under every climatic condition, in every part of the world. Yet a satisfactory theory of arch design was not proposed by Giovanni Polini until twelve centuries after the Fall of the Roman Empire. Today structural solutions are tested before the building is built. The engineer integrates all the varied physical factors of which he or she is aware before the builder breaks ground. Today's engineers are concerned primarily with innovation in the construction industry, which they visualize as an abstract problem. A modern engineer cannot afford to experiment, as did the classic engineers, by making smaller prototype structures. When an idea is committed to construction the engineer must be absolutely sure that it will work. If he designs a new structure, one that is unique and has never been built before, then he must create a new structural theory.

As recently as two decades ago, when engineers were required to analyze an untried structure, they often found calculations so complex that it was not uncommon practice to change the structure to simplify calculations. Today, with the aid of computers, mostly any structure can be accurately analyzed. The considerations that inspired the engineers of antiquity have reversed. The Romans used slave labor; materials were expensive. In contrast, labor is the precious ingredient today.

During the past years two design tendencies came into conflict. One was that of the search for more sophisticated building joinery and more precise tolerance, but the reduction of tolerance dictates very careful workmanship, which conflicts with actual field conditions. Building skills have deteriorated as industrial machine manufacturing capabilities have improved.

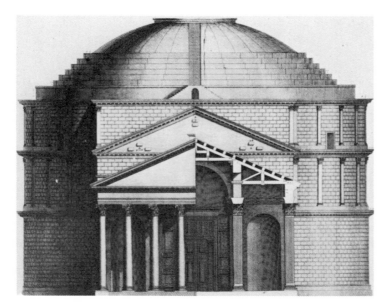

THE PANTHEON FROM THE LIBRARY OF THOMAS JEFFERSON
(Fine Arts Library, The University of Virginia)

STEEL STRUCTURE, CORNER DETAIL (Courtesy
of American Iron and Steel Institute)

The conflict between these two tendencies increases the importance of the engineer's decisions. The optimum reduction of field labor costs is as much a design inspiration to today's engineer as the manipulation of the classic forms of antiquity were to Renaissance architects. Larger and larger sections of the building are preassembled in factories and brought to the building site, which further reduces the demand on the dwindling skills of building labor.

Engineers try to make labor errors impossible. Increasingly more sophisticated assemblies are designed to be increasingly more simply assembled. As labor becomes less adept, it is designed around, and in turn rendered, the less skillful. As the process accelerates, the intelligence of work is more and more concentrated in the hands of designers, who, in turn, put more and more faith in computers and less and less in on-the-job decisions.

The design objective of buildings has shifted. A generation ago it was in the formal aesthetic of the designer. Today, form is of almost no importance. Spaces, cost, building time, and the technique of building assembly are the essential elements.

The evolution in construction technology, as in other technical fields, is in the hands of a limited number. The computer has revolutionized almost every operation for which it is used, yet computers are operated by push buttons. They require great skill to program and almost no skill to operate. The result is a series of technical cycles, in which each new invention solves an existing problem, but in so doing creates a new one. The new problem is of a higher level of complexity and requires a solution involving a higher technology, posing a still larger problem, which must be solved by a still higher level of technology. Invention has become the mother of necessity.[5]

Escalation becomes hypnotic and solutions are conceived only in terms of the technology that caused the problem. If schools are bad the tendency is to spend more money on them. If the welfare system fails, more funds are demanded for new welfare programs. If bombings are unsuccessful, then more and larger bombs are dropped. In building, the elevator cycle began with an increase in land values. To lower the unit cost of land, taller buildings were built. Land values increased and soon there was a need for improved elevators. Buildings got higher, the land values increased; and, as land values

WORLD TRADE CENTER (Courtesy of Otis Elevator Co.)

increased, more was paid for the land and taller buildings had to be built to justify the investment. Despite the problems of crowding, density, pollution, fire, noise, and congestion, it is impossible to think about a downtown without elevators. The solution becomes the problem.

With the use of the computer, problems can be solved that could not have been considered before. They demand increasing data complexity. Data is needed to acquire data. Yet the rich variety of measurements is limited to fit the computer. Some problems are solved and larger problems are created.

The technical myth that if our institutions increase in size they will become more efficient and will better serve their purposes ignores the unobtrusive sliding of major institutions into their present counterproductive activities. Counterproduction is locked into the agency that produces it. It is the paradoxical effect of a tool, a car, a school, a hospital, when its use achieves the opposite of what was intended.

On the one hand, the society encourages people to walk, learn, and heal; and, on the other, it institutes transportation, education, and medical care. Up to a certain threshold these activities are compatible, even mutually enhancing. Beyond that threshold too many cars are driven too fast, too many students take too many courses, too many patients occupy too many sickbeds, and these institutions become parasites sucking the autonomy from the walkers, the learners, and the actively healthy.

Our technologies, developed to achieve practical purposes, have passed the threshold of mutual help and turned malignant. The designer tied to the production system is helplessly committed to directing and manipulating techniques that destroy the ideals of health, safety, and welfare he and she are sworn to uphold.

During the final years of the dinosaur, it must have been evident, even to them, that they had pushed the lizard principle to rediculous lengths. One theory of evolution claims that the reptile kings succumbed to the attacks of shrewlike creatures that they could not combat because they were so small. The forerunners of the age of mammals, it is claimed, gnawed through the shells of dinosaur eggs and ate the dinosaurs' hope of survival.

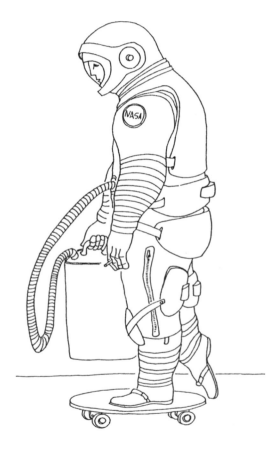

EduKation

Our systematic treatment of the building arts has reached the dinosaur proportion, of World Trade Centers. But evolutionary successors are gnawing away at the foundations. Evidences of change are found in discontinuity as striking as the difference between the brontosaurus and the mouse. The very size and ungainliness of our building efforts seems to hasten their end. The newly hatched eggs of World Trade Centers feel the sharp fangs of the shrew heralding a drastic change in evolution.

As the wire nail made every man and every woman a potential carpenter, the pocket calculator today makes every child a potential accountant and the CB radio makes every motorist part of an early-warning system. The housewife can now challenge the multi-million-dollar computers mobilized by the utility companies, and the motorist can elude the sophisticated network of radar, broadcasting stations, helicopters, and automatic weapons of the law. The concentration of engineering sophistication and simple assembly, devised to overcome field labor conditions on major construction projects, paves the way for the introduction of technically sophisticated building components in the home as consequential as the wire nail and hand calculator.

The chemical industry floods the market with mastics that can be used to join every imaginable material together, even people, as trips to emergency wards to separate joined fingers constantly remind us. This may be a mishandling of technology, but an entirely new potential for workmanship emerges.

If a computer can be operated by the push of a button, then ordinary people are as capable of pushing as hard as designers. As the spirals of technical cycles are broken, new combinations come into being. Plastic pipe puts plumbing technology within reach of bank clerks. The lumberyard, turned building-supply supermarket, delivers building materials to housewives, children, and home craftsmen. Their use violates all proprietary restrictions of organized labor, offends the aesthetic senses·of professional designers, and breaks almost every building code and ordinance. Yet it is the homecraftsman, woman, and child, not the industrial designer, that makes the housing product a home.

Do-It-Yourself Coffin Kits

Alternative Ways Of Burial Gaining

By Janis Johnson
Washington Post Staff Writer

When Judith Davis' mother-in-law died a year ago, the funeral director persuaded the family that an airtight metal casket would be most appropriate for her burial.

But Davis was unsettled by that experience. "I decided I didn't want that to happen to me. I have very strong feelings about wanting to return to the earth naturally," she said.

So Davis, now 40 and someone who doesn't expect to die for a long time, bought herself a pine coffin kit and became one of dozens of local residents to enter a fledgling movement aimed at providing alternatives to the contemporary American way of burial.

"I haven't put it (the coffin) together," said Davis, who lives in the District. "I want to do it with friends. That's not something you just pick up the phone and ask them."

Several weeks ago, a 14-year-old Bethesda girl who died of cystic fibrosis, was cremated in a pine coffin painted by artist Margo Newhouse of Potomac.

The girl's mother wanted something that represented her daughter's "spirit toward living." Newhouse explained. She painted the coffin in turquoise with a rainbow of red, orange, yellow, purple, blue and green extending around the sides and a butterfly on the lid.

"So many people thought it was just right," Newhouse commented.

The St. Francis Burial Society, a local group promoting simple, inexpensive and biodegradable coffins and cremation ash boxes is behind all this. They produce coffin kits, pre-assembled rectangular and mummy-style coffins and cremation boxes, all of pine. They also sell sturdy cardboard coffins and instructions for making a coffin from scratch.

What's more, the society, urges living with coffins rather than just getting buried in them. Blanket or toy chests, coffee tables, desk and tool boxes are among the uses they recommend. Paint, varnish and handcarve them or convert the boxes into a combination planter-bookshelf-wine rack, the society recommends.

Accompanied by a coffin during lectures on death and dying, the Rev. Robert Herzog, a St. Francis founder, has watched people eying the unfinished box cautiously. "They're intimidated by it. Then they begin to move their hands across the wood . . . How many times have you had that experience of knowing what you'll be in when you die?" he asked.

The pine coffin concepts harkens back to medieval Europe and colonial America when

The Rev. Vienna Anderson, left, stands next to own coffin.

See COFFINS, E4, Col. 1

Coffin's many uses includes as a wine rack.

The key to the inventive use of the technology that is developing, that bares the teeth of the shrew, is found in the use of technical products that encourages people to do things for themselves, rather than to depend on things done for them. It is difficult to anticipate the role of the designer that will emerge from this new relation to production. But we do know that the Eric Hoffers of this world will not continue to throw their cargo hooks, their backs, and their minds into moving crated "crap" forever.

footnotes

1. Samuel Lefrak - Interview in FORBES Magazine, December 15, 1974 (p. 23).
2. Harry Braverman - LABOR AND MONOPOLY CAPITAL, Monthly Review Press, N.Y.C., 1974 (p. 200).
3. Ibid., (p. 200).
4. Final report of THE NATIONAL COMMISSION ON PRODUCT SAFETY, issued June, 1970, Superintendent of Documents, U. S. Government Printing Office, Washington D.C.
5. Richard Bender - A CRACK IN THE REAR VIEW MIRROR, A View of Industrial Building, Van Nostrand Reinhold, N.Y.C., 1973.

MID-MANHATTAN STREET SCENE, 1978

SAN GIMIGNANO

55

THE CREATION

IN THE BEGINNING ...

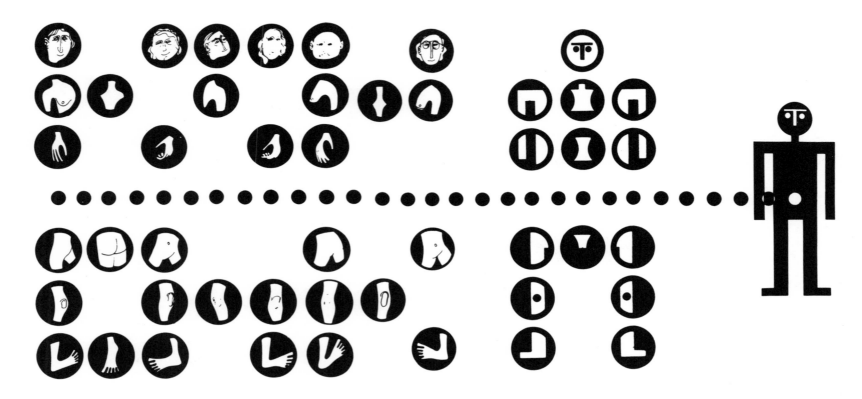

INDEPENDENT VARIABLE •••• STATISTICAL AVERAGE •••••••••MAN

UNIFIED UNISEX
A PERSON FOR ALL SEASONS

The steam engine freed humankind from the drudgery of physical work, the computer frees him from the drudgery of thought.
A. Farch

Systems

During the latter part of the 1930s a metamorphosis in the orderly progression of technical development took place. The first evidences of what was later to be variously termed "systems analysis, operational research, process and performance design" appeared when "efficiency experts" began conducting time/motion studies in the late 1930s. Scientists became the first practitioners of the new techniques, which were later to change the basic concept of design inherited from managing craft work to what is now termed "problem solving." In the transformation a good measure of the intelligence of work was shifted from designers to computer programmers.

The American Civil War is the historic marker that indicates the sharp division between craftsmanship and industrial design. Similarly, the Second World War is the dividing line between industrial design and problem solving. In this simplified capsulation of design history the draftsman's working drawing symbolically typifies the design in industrial management, and the programmer's diagram, the problem solving techniques of systems analysis. Both industrial management and systems analysis were born before the two wars, but wartime concentration on technology shaped their growth and impelled them toward maturity.

A link can be established between industrial management and systems analysis as the logical extension of the inventions of the Industrial Revolution, beginning with the spinning machine and ending with the computer. But this comparison does not adequately acknowledge the qualitative change that occurred in work. When people spun by hand the spinning machine performed some small, selective functions similar to those of the human brain; but the primary use of spinning machines was to duplicate the physical work of spinning. The function of computers is to calculate. Spinning duplicates human action; calculating duplicates human intelligence.

The first machines of the Industrial Revolution were magnifications of physical capabilities. They increased the craftsman's productivity. Water and windmills, using gear systems, converted the energy of falling water and wind pressure to energy that duplicated the actions of hand-held mortar and pestle, trip hammer, and the reciprocal strokes of the saw blade performed by the human arm.

HEIGHT FINDING RADAR AND RADAR SCOPES AND READERS
ON SAIPAN DURING WORLD WAR II
(Photos courtesy Office Of The Secretary Of Defense)

The steam engine converted fuel to energy, taking the place of wind and water to further magnify human muscle power. The intelligent craftsman was essential to their operation. Machines that extend human sensibilities, such as radar, sonar, television, and the computer, were not developed extensively until the thinking workmen who once directed muscle machines could be replaced by machines.

The invention of smart machines is a new phase in human-kind's productivity that has accelerated the division between intelligence and action in work. In a piecing together of the recent history of systems analysis, beginning with World War II, we find that most of the problems solved were military. Industrial and social problems are a comparatively recent development. In wartime Britain a group of physicists, electronic engineers, and related professionals were asked to devise ways to use newly invented radar. It was a logical choice since scientists were the original inventors. From that time on representatives of the various branches of the sciences were recruited to work together on wartime problems. With this successful precedent, systems analysis teams were consulted by the military on a regular basis. Operations research was born of war's increasingly complex scientific technology and equipment. Interdisciplinary teams were organized since members of the individual sciences had no previous experience involving such a wide range of cross-disciplinary problems. The English example quickly took root in the United States. Scientific teams worked on logistical problems during World War II, designing the proximity fuse, planning the sea mining of Japan, inventing the massed ship convoy and new flight patterns, among other achievements. Advanced research was conducted by the Federal Government as part of top secret defense operations and the stage was thus set for the postwar development of systems analysis and operations research in many fields.

The basic concepts of teamwork, scientific method, and sequential treatment of problem perimeters are ideally suited to concepts of research and investigative methods using computer and information retrieval devices. Operational research, systems analysis, or scientific problem-solving proliferated enormously after the Second World War. Almost no activity was untouched. It's growth is analogous to the all-encompassing expansion of industry and subsequent management techniques that took place after the American Civil War.

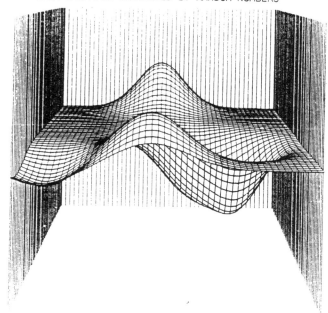

COMPUTER GRAPHICS GENERATED BY RANDOM NUMBERS

The instruments that systems managers and operational researchers use are extensions of human intelligence, and, therefore, impinge upon the activities of managers, designers, and decision makers at first and then eventually replace them. The new techniques convey the intelligence of work; the decision-making activities are further removed from the actual work performed. They codify and centralize the work into more specialized management. A metamorphic change occurs with attendant reverberations throughout the entire structure of design and work. We find a difference in kind rather than extent between the following statements. The first was made by Walter Gropius, architect and founder of the Bauhaus, when speaking of the machine in 1935; the second, by Negroponte, architect and researcher of MIT, when speaking of the computer in 1969.

...an instrument which is to relieve man of the most oppressive physical labor and serve to strengthen his hand so as to enable him to give form to his creative impulse....[1]

Negroponte's view is that of an equal partner:

Treat the problem as the intimate association of two dissimilar species (man and machine), two dissimilar processes (design and computation), and two intelligent systems (the architect and the architecture machine.)[2]

Gropius voiced the idealism typical of the modern movement in art early in the century. The French writer Paul Valery said, "A book is a machine for reading." Ozenfant called painting, "a machine for moving us." Le Corbusier termed the house, "a machine for living in." Eisenstein said, "The theater is a machine for acting"; Marcel Duchamp, "the idea is the machine for making art." All of these men conceived of the machine as more than the means of releasing humankind from the drudgery of work. It was a creative expedient. They expressed their dissatisfaction with the craftsmen who did not share their vision and labeled them selfish and egocentric guardians of the old order.

Ironically, programmers and those involved with systems design often categorize the attitudes of industrial designers in the same way. But, while artists rhapsodized over the machine and programmers praised the computer, the proponents of industrial management and systems design alike stated their objectives quite simply as those of maximizing return on investment.

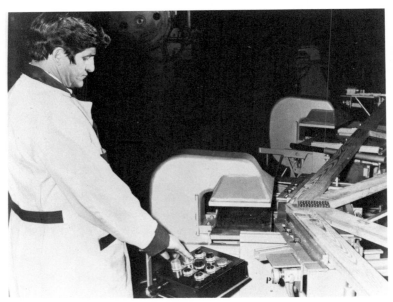

AUTOMATED LIGHT WOOD FRAME TRUSS NAILER
(Courtesy of Gang-Nail Corporation)

LEARNING LABORATORY,
NEW HAVEN GRAMMAR SCHOOL

Wrote Frederick Taylor in his principles set forth in
Scientific Management:

> *They [industrial managers] recognize the task before*
> *them as that of inducing each workman to use his*
> *best endeavors, his hardest work, all his traditional*
> *knowledge, his skill, his ingenuity, and his good*
> *will--in a word, his initiative so as to yield the*
> *largest possible return to his employer.*[5]

Wrote Thomas W. Maver of the Building Performance Research Unit,
University of Strathclyde, Glasgow in 1968:

> *Decision making in building design, as in many other*
> *fields of design and planning, is concerned with*
> *narrowing the field of search, in the universe of*
> *possible design solutions for the design which*
> *optimizes the return on the client's investment.*[4]

The objectives of the systems designers are analogous to those
formerly held by industrial management, but the end objective is
not industrial products, but the management of industrial thinking.
Christopher Jones describes the attitude as one which assumes the
design to be entirely explicable, even though practicing designers
may be unable to give convincing reasons for the decisions they make.
The inventors of most systematic design methods do not question the
idea that a human designer is capable of operating entirely ration-
ally with full knowledge of his actions. The picture projected is
that of a human computer operating only on objective information,
following a planned sequence of analytical, synthetic, and evalua-
tive steps and cycles, until the designer objectively realizes the
best solution.

Christopher Jones has described the attitudes that direct the
change of design from a craft to a manageable technology. It is
this metamorphosis that makes the position of the industrial designers of the built environment so difficult. For, despite the almost
universal application of operational research, systems analysis, and
performance design in science and industry, architects and all other
industrial designers continue to cling to their craft methods of
arriving at design decisions intuitively, by trial and error. They
do this in much the same way that industrial craftsmen clung to
their intuitive craft thinking when Taylor introduced the division
of labor that rendered their skills obsolete.

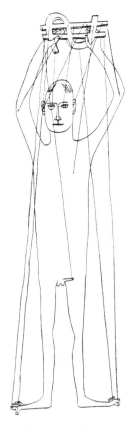

JET AIRCRAFT SIMULATION TRAINING DEVICES
(Photo courtesy of Goodyear Aerospace Corp.)

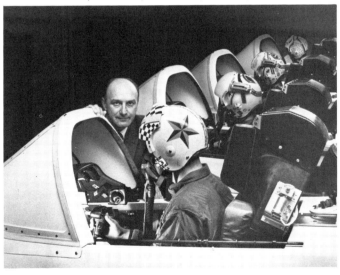

The intent of both scientific method and scientific management have been forthrightly declared as "management control." The one clearly defined continuum, from the power loom to the computer, from designer to programmer, is the strengthening and further centralization of this control.

Systems analysis is said to be a means of making objective decisions in which the designer is placed by the method above the frailty of his or her egocentric prejudices. The same virtue was attributed to machine operation in 1914. "Standardization to be understood as the result of a beneficial concentration, will alone make possible the development of a universally valid, unfailing good taste," declared Herman Mathesius.

Yet, despite good intentions that have persisted for over half a century, universal good taste has not materialized. Objectivity seems equally elusive; but there is some doubt that it ever did exist. The operational researchers of World War II were hardly objective; their intention was to bomb, burn, maim, and kill the enemy. The inherent contradictions in both ideals obviously are not the fault of industrial designers or programmers, but of the ideas themselves; for as good taste did not seem designable, objectivity does not seem programmable.

When designers or programmers classify people as objects to solve problems, people become objects. This was documented time and time again in the words of Studs Terkel's workmen. Any decision involving systems methodology, no matter what its scientific justification, cannot escape the ethical judgment of the designer. Absolute objectivity, which systems analysis claims to achieve, is no more attainable than Mathesius' universal good taste.

Every designer decides what the environment he seeks to create should do. This is not a question of design, but of ethics. The assumption of scientific methods is based on the idea that objective evaluations are possible. The subjective choice of criteria predetermines the context of the solution. Objective analysis is built upon a framework of criteria and standards against which achieved changes are measured by values applied by the designer at the beginning of the process. The choice of objective method is based on personal values. The designer selects mechanisms appropriate to the designer's view of the world. The mechanisms chosen may well reflect inadequate and unhealthy personal values, as well as healthy and beneficial ones.

CHOICE   CHOICE   CHOICE

CHOICE   CHOICE   CHOICE

CHOICE   CHOICE   CHOICE

CHOICE   CHOICE   CHOICE

CHOICE   CHOICE   CHOICE

CHOICE   CHOICE   CHOICE

CHOICE   CHOICE   CHOICE

CHOICE   CHOICE   CHOICE

CHOICE   CHOICE   CHOICE

CHOICE   CHOICE   CHOICE

CHOICE   CHOICE   CHOICE

CHOICE   CHOICE   CHOICE

CHOICE   CHOICE   CHOICE

CHOICE   CHOICE   CHOICE

CHOICE   CHOICE   CHOICE

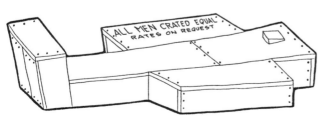

ALL MEN CRATED EQUAL
RATES ON REQUEST

The evidence seems clear that, applied to the human condition, objective analysis techniques create difficulties for humankind. This does not mean that their relevance for certain aspects of design problems is not valid, nor that they cannot be used beneficially in very abstract ways. The fundamental quality of the organization of problem solving is not even remotely comparable to the dynamics of human experience. No amount of manipulation of the process can overcome this basic shortcoming. If the designer tempers abstract relationships with actual human experience at all, this comes from the injection of personal experience to weigh the problem factors.

Problem-solving elements must be uniform. If they are not they are manipulated and rendered consistent by applying statistical methods. The wide range of human dimensions are averaged by the application of standard deviation techniques. Either giants or midgets are automatically eliminated. If we consider how the techniques constrain the individuals and limit freedom to choose experience for themselves, deviation in human behavior is not surprising. When the human being is analyzed as a bundle of tendencies or elemental drives to become components of design problems, the individual is automatically eliminated. Personal behavior can only be comprehensible as the expression of the totality of the human experience, which can neither be captured nor evaluated by the mechanisms used.

When one person classified "an other" as an object or social unit that will behave consistently with all objects of the class, he or she automatically categorizes himself and herself as an object in a class of objects which is not "the other." The "other" reciprocates; a spiral is established which is only broken with great difficulty and through an attempt to see the other as not an object. Architects coping with large numbers of people find this a difficult adjustment to make. They feel the need to adopt an objective and cumulative attitude because of the sheer magnitude of the problem. When this is done, the need to categorize increases the problem. The people designed for become the problem to which a solution is sought. They, as objects in the solution and in defense of their identity, reduce everyone else to the same objectives for whom they need feel no responsibility.

Lack of concern increases in direct proportion to the degree of generalization made about human beings. When goals are standardized, the group has no existence separate from the people who compose it. The group's consensus becomes the individual's perception, which leaves the individual less free to develop goals and personality.

APARTMENT HOUSE FACADES NEW YORK CITY
(Photo by F. Wilson)

NOTICE

PLEASE DO NOT ATTACH POSTERS, PICTURES, ETC., TO PAINTED WALLS, PANELED WALLS OR DOORS. THEY WILL REMOVE PAINT AND FINISH. A CHARGE WILL BE MADE WHERE DAMAGE WARRANTS.

DEFACING, REMOVAL OR OTHERWISE DAMAGING THIS SIGN WILL RESULT IN A $10.00 CHARGE.

The attempt to be objective in the human sphere becomes a means of evading moral responsibility for design decisions. Even when the designer attempts to find out what people want and to design an environment that will allow them to do it, the designer must decide whether to encourage or change their attitudes. When the designer decides upon a particular action it is an automatic decision that to decide is right and that not to decide is wrong. To decide not to decide is as much an expression of decision as is the decision to decide. No matter how far back the decision is taken, the result is always the same. It is a personal choice made on the basis of personal values for which responsibility cannot be abdicated. The responsibility for deciding to let people do what they want to do is unavoidably the designer's decision.

The theories of behavior upon which design decisions are based consider any form of deviance a statistical problem. A small minority of people are judged to be deviant because they are a minority. The concept of deviance is an administrative decision that ignores relevance, personality, and motivation. The person as such does not exist. There is no way of being absolutely certain that the deviant is not sane, and the society mad.

The values of the society, or the majority, are accepted as a starting point. At no time is the user visualized as the designer's equal. For example, it is never asked what kinds of questions he or she would like to answer. The user is given questions the designer wants answered. The individual's choice is eliminated by employing the analysis techniques of problem solving. Systems design implicitly discourages individuation and encourages the development of group identification and thus the formation of subcultures. Valuable sources of information about how people perceive their environment, such as newspaper clippings, prohibition notices, and symbolic reference in the existing environment, can be very explicit and are vital expressions of user perception. Yet, they do not find their way into the elements of the design problem.

The rightness or wrongness of the physical environment are personal issues. Analytical techniques, which originate in the context of absolute or deterministic notions, lead to dishonesty for the designer and alienation for the user. National standards are determined as the result of these analytical techniques. Those who lend money for building will not do so for unconventional building forms. Planning regulations limit the choice of site, tax rate assessments discourage improvement, tehant associations dictate the colors of doors and curtains. Prefinished industrial building components limit the range of internal finishes and the large furniture manufacturers reduce the choice of furniture to the wrappings.

WOODCUT FROM MAXIMILIAN'S TRIUMPHAL ARCH BY ALBRECHT DURER

ethic$

The statement concerning "ends and means," made by Archibald Cox speaking of the Watergate investigation, seems to offer some direction in the dilemma of deciding and not deciding:

> In each case, the conduct--the objective acts-- was wrong because it violated standards that must be accepted if free men are to live together. In each case, the actor believed his wrong to be justified by the righteousness of his cause and the need for drastic means to achieve his objective....
>
> One can never be sure of ends--political, social, economic. There must always be doubt and difference of opinion. There is not the same margin of doubt as to means. Here fundamentals do not change; centuries of thought have established standards. Lying and sneaking are always bad, no matter what the ends.
>
> The point seems vital. If man is by nature a social being, if we are destined to live and work together-- if our goal is the freedom of each to choose the best he can discern--if we seek to do what we can to move toward the realization of these beliefs, then surely some virtually absolute constraints upon the ways in which we pursue even the worthiest of objectives (insofar as their worth can then be judged) furnish the best, perhaps the only, hope of man....
>
> Disregard of the constraints of some breeds further disregard upon the part of others, brute power becomes the determinant of what is falsely labeled "justice." Many of the greatest wrongs known to history were committed by men who were acting, according to the contemporary judgment of society as well as their own lights, in the cause of truth and human welfare.

It seems the peculiar prerogative professionals assign themselves is that of overriding the constraints that Cox describes. The doctor feels he has the right to deceive us "for our own good." The artist makes arbitrary decisions contrary to the popular taste in the name of the higher morality of aesthetics, verified by the artists peculiar momentary stylistic passion. The "knowing better," the

U.S. FLAGS IN RELIEF EXECUTED IN COMPUTER GRAPHICS

BOEING B-17 FLYING FORTRESSES DROP BOMBS ON ENEMY INSTALLATIONS
(Official U.S. Air Force Photo, World War II)

making of decisions for others are rights professionals seek by becoming professionals. Yet disclosure, reason, and forthrightness are what we expect of human intercourse.

What are the peculiar moral principles involved in work that encourage the violation of the "standards accepted by free men if they are to live together" that Cox described so eloquently? It is obvious to all that unintended damage is done to humankind by human work. Frederick Taylor was an idealist, as were the artists of the modern movement and the members that compose the Design Methods Groupe, seeking to introduce rationality into the disorderly chaos of the design process. But no amount of idealism has protected the workmen from the "violence to spirit and body" described by Alexis de Tocqueville, Studs Turkel, and Saul Alinski.

John Stuart Mill seems to have said it best:

A state that dwarfs its men, in order that they may be more docile instruments in its hands, even for beneficial purposes, will find that with small men no great things can really be accomplished.

The words "work and "design" could be substituted for state; for states are founded and survive on work and their production systems.

The question to be answered by the use of operational research, systems analysis, and performance design seems a simple one. Are these methods, developed for the efficient dropping of napalm bombs indeed so "objective" that, by the manipulation of independent variables, we can transform "body counts" to "Home Sweet Home"?

footnotes

1. Walter Gropius - SCOPE OF TOTAL ARCHITECTURE, Collier Books (Harper), N.Y.C., 1943 (p. 22).
2. Nicholas Negroponte - THE ARCHITECTURE MACHINE, MIT Press, 1970, Cambridge, Mass. (Preface to the preface).
3. Harry Braverman - LABOR AND MONOPOLY CAPITAL, Monthly Review Press, N.Y.C., 1974 (p. 101).
4. Gary T. Moore, Ed. - EMERGING METHODS IN ENVIRONMENTAL DESIGN AND PLANNING, MIT Press, Cambridge, Mass., 1968, (p. 195).

I PROFESS

"I PROFESS"

THE WASHINGTON POST, MONDAY, NOVEMBER 6, 1978

Roger Rosenblatt

The Hated Professions

In the past few weeks I've seen two interviews on television which, I believe, reflect a national state of mind. One was with a fellow from an association of morticians, and the other was with an administrator from a medical association. As representatives of their respective professions, both men stood accused ion the grounds of some recent poll or book) of being crooks, cheats and liars. Both responded to the accusations in exactly the same way, by saying Oh, there may be two or three members of the profession who are unscrupulous, but on the whole you won't find a better bunch.

At these disclaimers, the interviewer scoffed openly, and you could feel a general scoff in the air. Clearly, he accurately represented the dim public view of both professions—just as he would have if his guests had been lawyers, cops or dentists. What has happened, it seems, is that most, if not all, lines of work have absorbed the class hatred that used to be reserved for religions and races. Oh, there may be two or three industrious postmen, but on the whole you won't find a lazier bunch.

It is, in fact, very hard to think of a single line of work today that is not despised by the general public, and despised in specific and individual terms. I offer the following chart, which lines up some jobs with their assigned characteristics:

clergymen	mush heads
lawyers	cheats
doctors	selfish cheats
insurance salesmen	swindlers
dentists	crooks
auto repair men	liars and swindlers
car salesmen	crooks and swindlers
politicians	crooks, swindlers and liars
pro athletes	babies
teachers	cowards
cops	bullies and crooks

And so on. One sure sign that these assigned characteristics are generally felt is the way certain lines of work are portrayed in fiction. Every writer who creates a clergyman-hero is sure to have him punch out someone at least once—as Father Karl Malden floored ex-boxer Marlon Brando in "On the Waterfront"—to show that men of the cloth are no pushovers. In the same

The Professions

The original meaning of the word "profession" was "to assume the vows of a religious order," but by 1675 the word had become secularized to mean "those who profess to be qualified." Profession, which originally defined the <u>act</u> of profession, has come to mean a vocation in which one professes to be skilled in the affairs of others or in the practice of an art based upon such knowledge.[1]

As labor became more stringently controlled, a group of men--managers, engineers, designers, and architects--became proficient in its management and direction. The theories of the modern artists, automation, and the beginning of the end of the Industrial Revolution had their origins in the dichotomy of work.

Historically, the term "professional" applied only to the three learned professions--divinity, law, and medicine. Today, from scientists to hit men, there are few vocations that do not claim or aspire to professional status.

The professions are near the top of the vocational hierarchy. Our most talented youths seek to enter them and the educational requirements are among the most demanding in the universities. Professional judgment is claimed to be based on altruism, public concern, and impartial judgment. Yet, despite these proud claims, it is painfully evident that we become less capable of coping with the problems that professionals profess to be able to solve.

Popular reaction to the disparity between professional claim and professional performance ranges from amused resignation to active resentment. The predominant moods are ones of fatalistic acceptance and anger manifested in a proliferation of liability claims.

Ironically, those who increasingly claim the title of professional do not, for the most part, base their claims on an improvement of their working skills, education, or personal or occupational development. The simpler tools have become through industrialization and automation, the more insistence there is in a professional monopoly on their use. Psychiatric social workers demand that simple conversation and common sense, when exercised by them, be awarded professional status and propose to prohibit its use by others.

By Charles Del Vecchio—The Washington Post

Margo St. James (back to camera) addresses conference at Capitol where her Coyote organization seeks legalization of prostitution.

Coyote Meets Here, Seeks Legalization of Prostitution

By J. Y. Smith
Washington Post Staff Writer

Margo St. James, a licensed private investigator who is also known as "The Coyote Trickster," went up to Capitol Hill yesterday and called for the legalization of prostitution in the name of women's rights.

"There are better ways to control this occupation than through the criminal justice system," she told a news conference.

Then she invited all members of Congress to a reception at the Wellington Hotel Thursday night to be hosted by the Hooker's Lobby and the First World Meeting of Prostitutes, which is scheduled to run from Wednesday through Sunday.

"The only ones who will stay away are the customers," she said about the reception, to which congressional spouses and staffers also are invited.

St. James, 38, is the founder and head of Coyote, which describes itself as " a loose women's organization" devoted to fighting for the civil rights of prostitutes.

The First World Meeting of Prostitutes and the Hooker's Lobby are being sponsored by Coyote together with the Feminist Party. Besides the congressional reception, highlights include the First International Hooker's Film Festival.

St. James, who said she was a prostitute for "eight or 10 years" beginning in 1962,

declared that the recent sex scandals involving congressmen make this a good time for her lobby to go to work.

"The perfect time to hit them is when their guard is down," she said.

She said she had met 14 women since she came to Washington from San Francisco last week who told her that they had had affairs with congressmen. She said some of them would address workshops of the forthcoming First World Meeting.

"I can't name the congressmen, nor would I," she said. "I feel that would be against my rules of integrity."

St. James said she became a prostitute after being arrested by "two policemen who came to my apartment in San Francisco, and I had never turned a trick in my life."

She said she finally won an appeal of her conviction, but that her arrest record made it virtually impossible for her to get any other line of work. Besides, she said, "I had to pay for my appeal."

St. James said her arrest record made it impossible for her to become a licensed private investigator in California until this year. She said her investigator's license "enhances my credentials as an expert witness."

She said she does some insurance work and some "police brutality cases" as a private investigator, but that she really support herself through speaking about prostitution.

By Charles Del Vecchio—The Washington Post

St. James now makes "a lot more talking about it."

NEWS STORY THE WASHINGTON POST JUNE 22, 1976

...the only proper authoritative body

They also demand pay and professional recognition for what friends and sympathetic bartenders give away. As contraceptive methods became almost foolproof, "Coyote," an organization of "loose women," and "The Hooker's Lobby" met in Washington D.C. to form the First World Meeting of Prostitutes. They petitioned the Congress of the United States to legalize the "world's oldest profession" in the name of women's rights.

Professionals seek the exclusive right to practice the arts in which they profess skill. In return the public allows professionals certain privileges in their practice, way of living, and thinking. The doctor is permitted to make life and death decisions for which the layman would be held criminally liable. The psychologist is permitted to ask personal questions that would offend normal social relations. The artist is allowed an egocentric sex life that would be labeled degenerate were he an auto mechanic.

Those who accept the professional's esoteric service do so in the belief that it is crucial to their well-being. The professional encourages this belief and will refuse to advise or perform services unless the recipient agrees to comply with his or her advice. The esoteric knowledge on which professional advice and action is based is seldom clearly defined and is often proposed in language that is incomprehensible to the layman, such as medical prescriptions, legal documents, and building specifications. Professional authority is based on the understanding that the advice given or action performed is derived from a branch of knowledge that the professional has mastered through initiation, apprenticeship, and concentrated study under masters who are also members of the profession.

It is assumed that the professional thinks objectively and advises clients on matters which they cannot themselves explore objectively due to their personal involvement. It is also understood that similar matters would be difficult for the professional to judge objectively if personally involved. As a consequence, it is considered unreasonable to ask the physician to heal himself or his family, the teacher to instruct his or her young, the architect to live in surroundings he or she defines as good design, or the psychologist to be a satisfactory parent.

The professional demands trust. The client is not considered capable of objective judgment and, therefore, is unfit to evaluate the services the professional renders. It is further tacitly agreed that the affairs of humankind are such that even the best professional advice and action will not always solve them. The recipient of

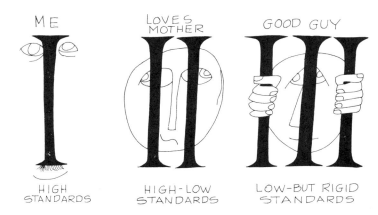

ME   LOVES MOTHER   GOOD GUY

I   II   III

HIGH STANDARDS   HIGH-LOW STANDARDS   LOW-BUT RIGID STANDARDS

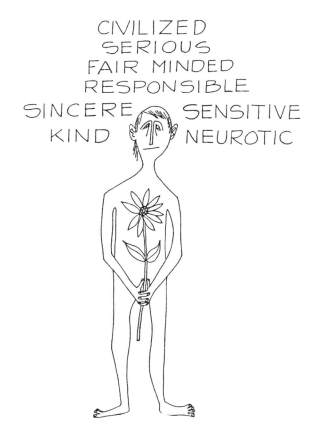

CIVILIZED
SERIOUS
FAIR MINDED
RESPONSIBLE
SINCERE   SENSITIVE
KIND   NEUROTIC

professional services is expected to suspend judgment and release the professional from responsibility for any unfortunate consequence of the actions. Professionals assert that only members of their own profession can judge them, and it is made extremely difficult for anyone outside their profession, even civil courts, to pass judgment upon one of their number.

Each profession's image of itself is that of the only proper authoritative body capable of setting the terms over which it professes esoteric knowledge. This mandate is implied in the practice of all professions, but granted more fully to some than to others. For example, the doctor's authority concerning life and death is considered more crucial than the architect's mandate over the quality of environmental aesthetics.

Lawyers serve their clients, but also develop a philosophy of law and justice. Physicians define the nature of disease and health and determine how medical services are distributed and paid for. Architects design buildings and seek to exert authority over urban design, regional planning, and the "quality" of the environment. As a consequence, the professional's field of esoteric knowledge tends to become an autonomous activity unrestricted by normal social constraints. We find Van Doesborg declaring as early as 1923 that "...art is free in the application of its means, but bound by its own laws and by nothing but its laws."[2]

Yet, in reality, professionals do not maintain an equilibrium between the universal and the practical. Although the priest may express an intellectual interest in all religions, he adhered to one to avoid a charge of heresy. The lawyer is interested in law generally, but his client's interest particularly. The architect may be vitally interested in aesthetic quality, yet adjusts his universal interest to fit his client's particular building needs. The balance varies. A measure of the universal and the particular establishes equilibrium between intellectual detachment and self-interest.

The introduction of professional study as an intellectual discipline in the university validates professional status. Study begins in undergraduate programs leading to a bachelor's degree with a major in the theory and practice of the vocation. The masters degree is the next step and becomes the standard professional qualification. This is sometimes extended to the Ph.D. Academic degrees which then become a qualification for higher administrative and teaching positions in professional agencies and schools.

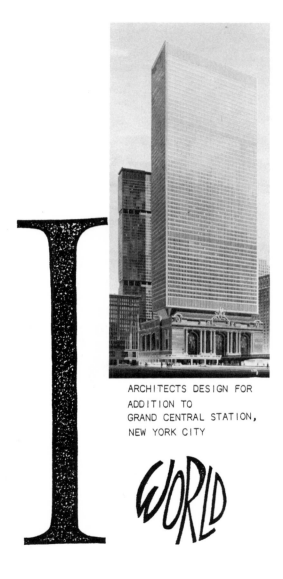

I WORLD

ARCHITECTS DESIGN FOR
ADDITION TO
GRAND CENTRAL STATION,
NEW YORK CITY

Solidarity among the members of a profession is reinforced and safeguarded so that a group apart is formed that develops its own ethos. Deep and lifelong commitment is demanded. A fully trained, licensed, and initiated professional who abandons the profession is considered a renegade by fellow professionals and, in the case of a priest, is considered a renegade in the eyes of laymen.

Professions tend to become manifestly culture bound. They may teach and advocate some universal truths, but surrounding this core of knowledge is a large body of practical experience relating only to one segment of the professional's particular culture. For example, a physician may be able to detect irregularities in the rhythm of the heartbeat of a South American laborer; yet he may lack even the slightest knowledge of how to advise him to accept the diagnosis and live with the ailment. The professional may well have become so accustomed to his or her particular way of practicing, payment, and division of labor that he or she will not and cannot adapt to the peculiarities of other societies. This is particularly true of professional relations with preindustrial or illiterate societies, as well as with disadvantaged groups in the professional's own society.

The measure of the individual professional's success is the magnitude of the problems he or she professes to solve. Successful architects become urban designers; unsuccessful architects design small shops, warehouses, work for developers, and occasionally design a private house. Successful university professors research; novice instructors teach. Successful physicians transplant human hearts; unsuccessful general practitioners work themselves to death saving lives threatened by the world's commonplace illnesses.

As vocations specialize, more conditions are defined as requiring specialized treatment. Workers cannot declare themselves sick without a doctor's approval, nor is a person dead until declared legally so under the conditions and circumstances the medical profession has chosen to define as death. The professional attitude or mood is characteristic of all highly industrial societies irrespective of political ideology. Old and new vocations endeavor to change their manner of work, relation to clients, the public, and their images of themselves to merit professional status. Computer data processors and medical specialists are among the most recent. In architecture the interior designer and those who plan and plant have become the interior architect, the city and urban planner, and the landscape architect.

Building product manufacturers have banded together to form "institutes" that disseminate information describing their particular products. Salesmen become "architectural representatives" and many hold "professional" architectural and engineering degrees. They profess to give impartial advice concerning the virtues of their particular products.

As medicine becomes more complex, the physician delegates more technical functions to the nurse, who in turn relegates them to practical nurses, aides, and maids. The nurse then seeks a measure of independence, prestige, and money in keeping with her changed duties. The vocational guidance worker petitions the teaching profession to recognize that his or hers is a separate complex of skills and asks to become a member of the academic faculty.

Vocations use the following criteria to justify their bid for professional status:

1. Altruistic public service.
2. Long and specialized training.
3. A code of ethics.
4. Meetings of professional members.
5. Journals devoted to improving the profession.
6. Examinations as barriers to entry.
7. Tacit prohibition against advertising services.
8. Practice of the profession limited to members who have been licensed or certified by an association made up of members of the profession.
9. Symbolic costumes such as black robes or white coats.
10. Control of the access and behavior of nonmembers in work places such as courts, classrooms, and sanctuaries.

But it is not for the purpose of wearing unique costumes or membership in exclusive clubs that vocations seek to attain professional status. They actually seek:

1. Autonomy, which means freedom from supervision on their jobs.
2. Individual recognition in their particular field of work.
3. Power to judge who is in their occupation and who is not; monopoly over their work, which frees it from interference from their employers and the general public.
4. Exclusive power to discipline wayward colleagues who deviate from their work ideology. Those who petition for professional status do not wish any outside agency to exercise such power over them.

CAST PLASTER CEILING
(Courtesy of Metropolitan Life Insurance Co.)

OBJECTIVE THINK

The desire for the autonomy to perform their jobs as they and they alone see fit motivates members of an occupation to seek professional status. Although many occupations attempt to attain professional status, most are doomed to disappointment. True professional status rests upon an implied relationship which is seldom discussed by either those who have attained professional status or those who try to acquire it.

"Intimidation is the essence of all professional relationships,"[3] says Dr. William Haga. This refers to the professional's ability to frighten whatever audience threatens his or her autonomy, whether these are employers, clients, or other outsiders. In the world of work only fear gets and keeps autonomy. A professional simply has authority over others and is, in turn, free from the authority of others.

When the members of a vocation resort to reason, persuasion, or argument, an equality of status between the two parties is implied. Argument or rational persuasion does not suggest an authoritarian relationship and is, therefore, unprofessional. When a practitioner must rely upon these means, it constitutes evidence prima facie that he or she is not a professional. A professional will make considerable effort not to fall back upon his power. However, in the last resort, the professional need not be rational, but simply threaten the withdrawal of services.

Intimidation is established by two factors--cruciality and mysticism. The person who seeks the advice of a professional must feel that the situation is crucial. He or she must also think that the professional has mysterious esoteric knowledge, skills, and powers the client cannot comprehend. Obscuring knowledge is, therefore, a professional objective. If the situation is not crucial and the professional's knowledge and actions not mysterious, the client cannot be intimidated and, therefore, a professional relationship cannot be established. An occupation has become a profession only when it can rely upon intimidation as its ultimate, if unseen, means of controlling others at work. Members of a profession have status because intimidation is effective. Vocations seek a unique personal status to establish identity in a work environment where anonymous interchangeability of human beings, like machine parts, is the normal condition.

Roman Architect XLII AD

He who appears before you now- is the Toad of this Thicket.

Master Mason 1250

Registered Architect 1980

the profession of architecture

James Howard Means claimed, "The behavior pattern of any profession does not develop overnight; it takes time to evolve. Its characteristics and configuration are formed by its environment and its heritage, as are those of a species in the course of its evolution."[4]

In the United States an advanced industrial, technological society took shape in the years following the Civil War. Work skills were increasingly specialized, finally resulting in the assembly-line worker at one extreme and the professional at the other. Although the American Medical Association had been formed before the Civil War, the American Bar Association did not emerge until 1878. Engineers formed a society in 1871 and then quickly divided into mechanical and electrical engineering associations in the 1880s. Seventy-nine professional societies were chartered in the 1870s and in the 1880s another 121 were added. The 1890s saw the formation of forty-five more. Frederick Taylor's experiments, which culminated in the assembly line, were begun at Bethlehem Steel in the 1880s, and in the 1890s he began to lecture, read papers, and publish the results of his work. As the old apprenticeship system in architecture declined, the American Institute of Architects was formed in 1857. The founding of the first professional school of architecture occurred at MIT in 1886, rapidly followed by schools at Illinois, Cornell, and Syracuse.[5]

In 1869 Mr. A. J. Bloor, secretary and archivist for the AIA, pointed out the need for organization:

However else American Architectects may differ, none of us surely can blind our eyes to the fact that we cannot, isolated, yield each other the support that we may if we stand all over our common country on a common platform of professional principles. We need our special platform from which to train the public... while at the same time, we protect ourselves from the jealousy, the misunderstanding, and ignorance of each other, of our clients, and of mechanics.[6]

Daniel H. Burham called for a code of ethics in 1887 that would define "especially what is professionally damnable" in architects dealings with each other.

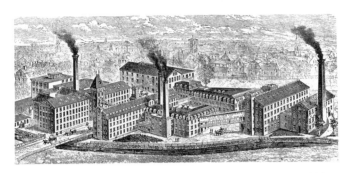

AMERICAN SCREW CO. MILLS, PROVIDENCE, R.I. CIRCA 1886

THE OLD SOUTH CHURCH, BOSTON, MASS., CIRCA 1889

Architecture seeks to serve the entire range of social pocess

The crucial element of the architectural profession was established when the AIA was called upon to adjudicate conflicts in contracts between practicing architects and the federal government. In 1886 the AIA ruled that it would act as mediator for its own members only, thus monopolizing itself as the only official representative body for the practice of architecture. The architects organized the practice of architecture in the same manner as did entrepreneurs in other fields of the economy. It was during this same period that Mr. Rockefeller was attempting to establish a "gentlemen's agreement" in the oil industry to impose order upon the chaotic conditions of competition.

Architecture is termed both an art and a profession. It is doubtful that a truthful definition would validate either definition of an activity organized as a corporate enterprise. As an art, architecture is concerned with practical problems. "Its content is social process," as James Marston Fitch pointed out, "which cannot be manipulated for the purely formal ends fine arts seek to achieve."[7] The slower building process cannot match the rapid series of seasonal enthusiasms that have characterized the fine arts during recent decades. Abstract expressionism, Pop, Op, Hard Edge, and over the edge to happenings have succeeded each other in less time than it takes to plan and place the foundations of a moderately sized office building.

As professionals, architects have contributed their share of mysticism to justify their activities, and, although they had attempted to monopolize the art of building during the latter part of the nineteenth century, they never acquired enough intimidating power to do so. The vocation of architecture lacks the crucial elements essential to achieve truly professional status.

The architect often appears in the public eye to be as much of a buffoon as the fine artist. Architects are also pictured as extravagant, irresponsible dreamers. The failure of architects, who have been the apologists for industrial technology, to build the bright new radiant cities they envisioned in the 1920s has led to the blaming of them for all the environmental failures of industrial technology. In reality architects have had little to do with the development of modern technology and exercise little control over technical decisions. The profession is blamed for the critical condition of the built environment, but exercises no crucial influence over it.

495. Chestnut St., Philadelphia, Penn., north side from Sixth to Seventh Sts., c. 1879.

CHESTNUT STREET PHILADELPHIA, NORTH SIDE
FROM SIXTH TO SEVENTH STREETS CIRCA 1879

CHESTNUT STREET PHILADELPHIA, SOUTH SIDE
FROM SEVENTH TO EIGHTH STREETS CIRCA 1879

494. Chestnut St., Philadelphia, Penn., south side from Seventh to Eighth Sts., c. 1879.

Architecture seeks to serve the entire range of social processes, from the monumental to the mundane. As a result, two contradictory value systems emerge. One derives from art, the other from science and technology. The combination is responsible for the richness of architectural education and the schizoid nature of the architect's professional problems.

Until the recent introduction of scientific problem-solving, architects positioned themselves closer to the artist than to the scientist. The architect sought to resolve the contradictions between form and content and in this resolution create a work of aesthetic value. The conflict between the formal requirements of the container and the functional requirements of the humans contained has traditionally been resolved in favor of the container. The architect employs a private symbol system, shared by other architects and transmitted through professional magazines and critics, to assess the value of his work. It is, for the most part, a dialogue between critic and architect with little interest for either the client or the user of the buildings.

Status and recognition for the architect are not contingent on performance judged by the consumers. Critics and fellow professionals decide the merits of the architect's work. The criteria used often differ radically from those of the client or the user of the spaces. There is no method by which the user can state his or her complaints and no mechanism by which the architect can receive feedback regarding the consequence of the design. Architects frequently receive recognition for designs that are judged failures by the building's users. This contradiction has always been present in the practice of architecture, but is now complicated by the increase in social, economic, and industrial processes that buildings now accommodate.

Although the architectural profession resembles that of law and medicine, architects have less control. Civil Engineers are licensed and qualified by virtue of their education to compete with architects. Structures such as bridges, highways, airports, dams, and seaport facilities are almost exclusively designed and built by engineers; and the structure of the buildings that architects design, as well as the mechanical, electrical, and plumbing systems, are invariably designed by engineers. In the comparatively new field of energy conservation solar energy engineers have assumed the major role. Architects merely give form to their concepts.

ENTRANCE TO GRADE SCHOOL, NEW HAVEN, CONNECTICUT, 1968

PAPER FLOWER ON
SCHOOL WALL

City, regional, and urban planning have developed into particular specialties known as the "planning professions." They compete with architects for commissions. The interior design of buildings is now a separate vocation demanding professional status for its members. Managerial firms increasingly assume the programming functions once performed by architects, and construction managers compete with architects for the title of master builder. Home building, the most important economic segment of the building industry, uses almost no architectural services. In small towns and rural areas individuals can and do design and build their own homes and small structures, unrestricted by the requirements of architectural and engineering approval.

As architectural offices evolved into corporate entities, the individual architect became a specialist. In large architectural firms architects concentrate on one aspect of one particular building, such as the curtain walls of skyscrapers, school furniture, the space planning of offices, or hospital facilities. The functioning architectural office was aptly described by Robert Sommer, Professor of Psychology and Chairman of the Psychology Department at the University of California at Davis:

> *The modern architectural firm is a bureaucratic monster designed to cope with the bureaucracy-- corporate as well as governmental--with whom it must deal. At the heart of the architectural giant is a computer surrounded by departments of architectural systems and research. One step removed from this are the category teams dealing with commercial buildings, educational buildings, public housing, and so forth. These are the real design groups who develop the specifications for each category of building. Their findings are used by the specific project teams working on individual jobs....In the past the teams could be small, consisting of an architect and a few skilled workmen. Now the teams can be extra- ordinarily large and will include a design group, structures people, sales specialists, sewage system analyst, town planners, as well as economists, sociologists, and environmental biologists....Many architects who have joined large construction firms or investment houses are indistinguishable from other corporate employees.*[8]

H.H. RICHARDSON ON COVER OF
PROGRESSIVE ARCHITECTURE

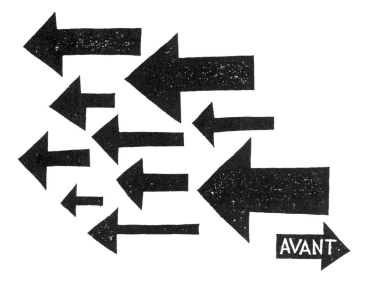

The paradox of Sommer's description is that practitioners nostalgically romanticize themselves as artist craftsmen while firmly organized along the corporate lines of industrial management. The architect's clients have specialized, defined programs and often have their own "in-house" architects, engineers, analysts, and computer programmers prepare the program given to the architect while their "in-house" professionals police his work. The architect's real client is no longer his legal client. The white collar worker in the skyscraper office, the industrial worker in the factory, the housewife in the housing project, the child in the consolidated school are the people for whom the architect designs and to whom he or she is ultimately responsible. Yet these are the people the designer never sees.

The architect deals with their representatives, corporate and institutional managers and executives. The designer does not design for real people, but rather to satisfy statistical data such as peak loads, median incomes, average family size, minimum floor areas. This data may be essential for establishing broad lines of policy, but is no more a substitute for firsthand knowledge about the actual user than are the statistics of the incidence of cancer to the physician treating a real patient. The result of this isolation from those who use the places architects design is an increasing emphasis upon the abstract and formal in architectural and urban design.

The architects social position is also unique. It is that of a respectable bohemian economically situated as a small, medium, or sometimes large businessman. Architects are thus economically insulated against the squalor and discomfort of the "culture of poverty" and are intellectually isolated from the social and cultural values of the middle class. Architects traditionally have depended upon the patronage of affluent groups and have identified themselves with them rather than the mass of ordinary people.

Although there is a tradition of social consciousness and intellectual commitment to social change among architects in the United States, which was voiced by Jefferson, Latrobe, Greenough, Sullivan, Wright, Gropius, and Neutra, it has been predicated upon utopian ideals, art, design, and form. The architectural profession has spawned no Gorkis to speak for those in the lower depths. Architectural services for low and moderate income groups, unless subsidized, are performed by students or an occassional idealistic egocentric.

BUILDING TRADES PICKET IN FRONT OF TISHMAN
BUILDING, NEW YORK CITY, 1967 (Photo by F. Wilson)

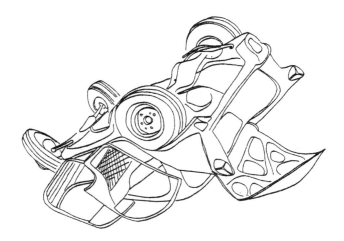

The revolutionary architectural prototype, Howard Roark of Ayn Rand's book, The Fountainhead, is revealing. The creative hero of this work, which strongly influenced young architects for at least a decade, gave vent to his revolutionary fervor by raping the heroine and dynamiting a building aesthetically offensive to him. This is hardly a description of "Mother Courage."

The architectural profession, like others, was involved in the New Deal and participated in government-sponsored projects during the depression of the 1930s. The architect's attention was momentarily turned to the problems of social architecture. However, the Second World War and the affluence that followed restored the architect's clients and with them the architect's faith in prevailing economic, political, and social institutions. Until the recent economic decline of the 1970s, the profession operated contentedly as a respectable element of the American business establishment. Architects have themselves become major businessmen and the American Institute of Architects has attempted through numerous seminars and publications to improve the position of architects in the business community. Except among those remnants of the counterculture now approaching middle age, the utopian element in architectural thinking, action, and the eccentric life-style, has largely disappeared.

The architectural profession centered in the university has made an extreme adjustment which has tended to eliminate the conventional wisdom of the preindustrial builder and the craftsmanship of the early industrial mechanics. Very few architects have first-hand knowledge of construction methods and techniques. In liability claims brought against architects almost all are against building failures; none have been lodged against building design.

The historic skills of the building craftsman are no longer required. Factory production, building components, and the mechanization of the construction industry have eliminated the need for the traditional intelligent, well-trained craftsman. The architect's working drawings and specifications intentionally prohibit on-the-job decisions by workmen.

When Studs Terkel's spot welder, Jim Grayson, says, "They have a better idea, they have better ideas of getting all of the work possible out of your worn body for eight hours," it is not surprising to hear Grayson also say, "There are specifications, which we pay very little attention to....you have inspectors who are supposed to check every kind of defect. All of us know those things don't get corrected....Whenever we make a mistake, we always say, 'Don't worry about it, some dingaling'll buy it.'"[9]

MOYAMENSING PRISON FORTRESS,
CIRCA 1876

HAYES HIGH SCHOOL FORTRESS
FIFTH STREET, CINCINNATTI, OHIO,
CIRCA 1876

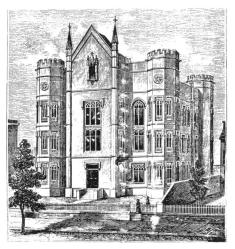

Little imagination is required to extrapolate the results of assembly line indifference into the statistics of highway death. Automobiles are designed and manufactured in a work process that makes accidents inevitable. Our built environment is assembled with the same worker indifference as are modern automobiles with one major exception--the "dingaling" does not have the privilege of choice. The growing evidence of inefficiency, waste, and frustration, the malaise of the institutional worker, and the active sabotage of the industrial worker of industrial products do not find their way into industrial design models. All design, like automobile design, is accident-prone.

The modern office building is designed so that is is only possible to work in it but one way--the way has been established by virtue of the design of its work positions. The geometry of the space and the location of energy outlets prevent any but specialized fixed activities. The designer must design schoolrooms that enable one teacher to dominate a group of passive students in front of a blackboard. Hospitals are designed as medical workshops where the patient is shelved to await the convenience of medical craftsmen. The form of the office building, the classroom, and the hospital are no more the result of the architect's design decision than Jim Grayson, the spot welder, can assure the safety of the driver of the automobile he welds on the assembly line. The architect, like Jim Grayson, is an implementor, rather than an originator, of design decisions.

These are decisions made by the society that supports the specialists who write the programs that direct the architect. The designer who claims responsibility for the quality of the built environment in reality only formalizes the dictates of institutional clients whose concern for humankind's well-being is limited to the extent that humankind's well-being coincides with institutional objectives. When an architect designs a prison, he or she does not question the system of justice that makes prisons necessary. Classrooms and hospital rooms are designed with no questions about the systems of education and medical care which mandate that hospital and classrooms be very much akin to prisons.

The overwhelming majority of architects solve only those problems assigned to them by institutional clients. They give form to mass institutional environments. Institutions are characterized by standardization. Standardization as a value is applied to all aspects of institutional environments, which is the means by which the institution asserts and maintains its authority and economic viability.

SEARS TOWER, CHICAGO BY ARCHITECTS SKIDMORE, OWINGS AND MERRILL (Photo by Ezra Stoller courtesy of Skidmore, Owings and Merrill)

TYPICAL LOWER FLOOR

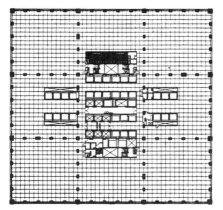

The architect works with the real clients, those who actually use the building less than one percent of the time and most commonly as an individual housing or personal building service which has very little general effect upon the community. The design professions are organized in such a way that profit is accrued in an inverse ratio to the amount of attention paid to individual human variables. Successful multimillion-dollar design firms that plan towns and cities may employ one hundred supporting specialists to every one designer. The ratio of person designed for to designer may easily approximate one to one hundred thousand. On the other hand, an independent architectural firm that designs homes for individual clients, does so with one or two designers and one or two draftsmen. The relation of person designed for to designer can be as low as one to one.

In keeping with the general reduction of personal service typical of all industries, from vending hamburgers to computerized banking, design services must be standardized to be profitable. Tremendous resources are required to build buildings as the industry is now organized. Institutions that command these resources care- fully safeguard their position. As a consequence, the professional architect does not exert an innovative influence on the built environ- ment nor can social innovation be accomplished by these architects.

The profession cannot offer viable alternatives to the client's revulsion against the patterns he or she imposes. Architecture reinforces industrial standardization because the profession has incorporated itself as an industrial entity and shares the moribund characteristics of other industrial institutions. The industrial capitalists and professionals that organized themselves to monopolize their interests at the end of the nineteenth century have fallen on hard times. In the words of Michael Harrington:

> ...[They] have become tamed, much less inventive, much less productive. The old entrepreneurial system was brutal, violent, repressive but it accomplished wonders. It built cities rather than destroyed them. It built railroads rather than run them into the ground. Now the minuses of capitalism remain and the pluses that came from creative brutality are not there any more on the same scale.

The profession of architecture today has very little to do with "art of building." In fact, architects no longer profess to be master builders, but instead rely upon their esoteric professional knowledge. Cruciality and mysticism may be fine elements upon which

FAVELA DA ROCINHA, SQUATTER HOUSING,
SAO CONRADO, BRAZIL

FAVELA DO TIMBAU, SQUATTER HOUSING,
PRAIA DE INHAUMA, FUNDAO, BRAZIL

are satisfactory qualities upon which to build a rule of law or a healthy society. They also lack the load-bearing qualities necessary to build buildings.

In fact, all that we have discussed here concerning the profession of architecture has a great deal to do with the profession and very little to do with the "art of building," which is the definition of architecture. The two, building and the profession of architecture, are not necessarily connected any more than law, health, or faith are dependent upon the priesthood or the Bar or Medical Associations. The ideals of religion, medicine, law, and architecture are not always best served by those who profess to be their guardians. The shepherd of the Christian faith is symbolically concerned with the welfare of his flock. A real life shepherd values his sheep for their wool and their mutton. From the sheep's point of view the shepherd's concern is, at best, hypocritical. The profession of architecture has difficulty in adjusting itself to the emerging idea of client autonomy just as few shepherds could tolerate the idea of a freewheeling lamb. The vocation of shepherding and all of its esoteric skill and knowledge is predicated upon herding sheep. The same techniques would be useless in herding bears, weasels, or mountain goats.

It is the assumed sheeplike character of ordinary people that encourages professionals to view them as statistics. But people do not consider themselves sheep. There is a growing tendency for people to be their own bears. This calls for an entirely different form of shepherding. It is one that is immeasurably more exciting, dangerous, and infinitely more satisfying than herding statistics.

footnotes

1. Kenneth S. Lynn and the Editors of Daedalus - THE PROFESSIONS IN AMERICA, Beacon Press, Boston, 1963.
2. Paul Overy - DE STIJL, Studio Vista, London, 1969 (p. 48).
3. William James Haga - CAN AN ENGINEER JOIN A UNION AND STILL BE A PROFESSIONAL? Austronautics and Aeronautics Magazine, Dec., 1975 (pp. 30-52).
4. James Howard Means - THE PROFESSIONS IN AMERICA, Beacon Press, Boston, 1963 (p. 47).
5. Laurence B. Holland - WHO DESIGNS AMERICA, Princeton Studies in American Civilization No. 6, 1965 (pp. 67-73).
6. Ibid., (p. 72).
7. James Marston Fitch - THE PROFESSIONS IN AMERICA, Beacon Press, Boston, 1963 (p. 231).
8. Robert Sommer - PERSONAL SPACE, The Behavioral Basis of Design, Prentice Hall, Englewood Cliffs, N.J., 1969 (p. 6).
9. Studs Terkel - WORKING, Avon, 1972, N.Y.C., (p. 229).

CHUTZPAH

The Architecture of Arrogance

The image artists, poets, and architects cherish of themselves is that of Renaissance men. This fantasy is vitally significant for it has persisted for five hundred years.

The peculiar form of Renaissance man, so beloved of artists, was fabricated by Florentine merchants during the fourteenth and fifteenth centuries. As a result of this veneration bestowed on them and men of their ilk, creative talent achieved an entirely new and unique social status in history.

Seven years before Francesco Petrarca was crowned laureate in Rome, the first poet to be so honored in modern times, the civic authorities of Florence elected Giotto di Bondone to the post of Master Mason.[1] It is doubtful that Giotto, a very fine painter, knew very much about stone cutting.' He was honored as a mason because, in the words of the city fathers that elected him, it was important above all else that the city architect be a famous man.

Although some Renaissance architects were indeed competent builders, it was no longer required that they be steeped in the craft of building to be recognized as great architects, as were their medieval predecessors.

The belief that artistic sensibilities are interchangeable and superior to all others is unique in history and not held by all people. We learn from Joseph Campbell that the Jacarilla Apaches of New Mexico assigned their artists to a taboo breaking clown society. Their bodies were smeared with white clay accompanied by four black horizontal stripes across their legs. They were termed "striped excrement."[2]

The Zeitgeist of the Renaissance that entitled artists to such extraordinary privilege is also unique to history. Medieval Masons learned their skills in the workshops as ordinary apprentices. During a period of three hundred years, from 1050 to 1350, medieval builders in France alone are claimed to have quarried more stone than the Egyptians during the three milleniums of their history. With it they built the magnificent cathedrals we now admire. Yet these builders remained remarkably humble throughout the entire three centuries of accomplishment. Remarkably few of the hundreds of magnificent churches, cathedrals, and monasteries they erected bear any acknowledgment of their authorship.

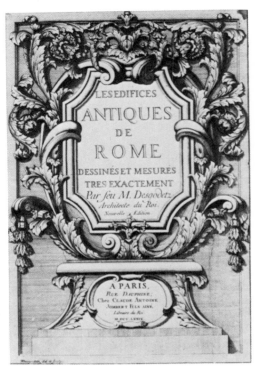

PAGES FROM BOOKS IN THOMAS JEFFERSON'S LIBRARY
(Courtesy of Fine Arts Library, University of Virginia)

PAGE FROM WORKBOOK OF THE INTERNATIONAL
CORRESPONDENCE SCHOOLS, SCRANTON, PA., 1893

Hammurabi, as you will recall, did not consider architects very special. His eye for an eye and tooth for a tooth code did not place a premium on talented molars. He numbered them one for one in retribution. The aristocratic Greeks had a high regard for beauty, but a low regard for work. The artifacts of Greek artisans were highly revered, but the artisans themselves, as often as not, were slaves. The Roman architect Vitruvius, famous for his Ten Books of Architecture, and, judging from his writings, a master builder, comes off historically as a sub-serviant, job-seeking, suppliant in his pleading preface of that famous work addressed to Cesar Augustus.

It is understandable that, in contrast to the status they have held during most of history, the Florentine concept of the artist as a divine, free-spirited, privileged, independent is one that artists are most anxious to promote.

Yet the extremely favorable social climate enjoyed by the Renaissance artists can only marginally be attributed to their genius. Their elevated status was as much a by-product of the Florentine merchant's bid for power as it was a tribute paid their work. The Medici, the Petti, the Rucellai, and the Strozzi families, although very important citizens, were in effect commercial upstarts on the historic scene. As an emerging merchant class they were engaged in competition for social privilege with the hereditary feudal nobility. They were badly in need of a corporate image, which in the age before the development of printing, radio, and television could only be supplied by artists.

The technique the Florentines employed is a familiar one found throughout history and used by powerful upstarts when ignored by the reigning society. A parallel cultural system is constructed. The Florentine merchants accomplished this by resurrecting the culture of antiquity to compete with the established signs and symbols of the medieval church. The unique attribute of this accomplishment was the unparalleled exploitation of artists and their works. Their triumph can be measured by the longevity of the architectural sign language evolved, which has persisted for five centuries and remains in good currency.

The forms of antiquity, found in the temple architecture of the Greek world and in the religious, military, and civil architecture of the Romans were resurrected and rearranged to compose the "Renaissance style." Archaeology and history became essential supports of architecture, as architecture was

SAN FRANCISCO, CALIFORNIA　　NORTHERN NEW MEXICO

PLAINFIELD, NEW JERSEY　　HELSINKI, FINLAND

forcibly altered from a building to a literary art. The classical language was accepted, developed, and persists in books and buildings to this day as the common symbol system of cultured taste the world over.

The elements are easily recognized. Columns of five standard varieties are applied in standard ways. Although arrangements are continually varied, adjusted, and departed from, they remain recognizable throughout all buildings termed "classical." Even departures from and reactions against the system--mannerism, Baroque, Rococo, and all their variations--used these familiar signs and symbols, cut and rearranged, made larger or smaller, as style and whim demanded. Even today we find service stations and tract houses decorated with bits of Renaissance memorabilia, and "classical" moldings and trim can be purchased at any lumberyard by any home craftsman. It is little wonder that these lingering symbolic reminiscences continually awaken artists toward recapturing their former glory.

Following the Renaissance artists have searched in vain for the fortunate coincidence of social situation, country, people, and historical tradition that would restore the importance they formerly enjoyed in Tuscany. It was not until the turn of the twentieth century that such an opportunity seemed to emerge. The imagination of artists, architects, and poets was fired by industrial power, machines, raw energy fun, profit, and the possibility of a comeback.

The time seemed once again propitious to materialize cultural icons and forge a culture for an emerging class, as had been done five centuries before in Tuscany. In defense of this artistic vision there has probably been no other group in history so badly in need of a cultural veneer as the industrial and manufacturing robber barons of the nineteenth century. The industrialists of Europe had followed imperialist armies throughout Africa and Asia and built their industrial might on the mineral wealth and rural products of conquered agrarian nations. The industrialists of America had exploited the resources of a continent in timber, minerals, oil, and land in record time. Opposition to working conditions had been raised to the statue of social revolution. Capital punishment for destroying lace frames was reintroduced in England, during the earlier part of the nineteenth century, and pitched battles between coal miners and Pinkertons were fought in the Pennsylvania coal fields late in the same century. Everywhere industry and manufacturing were victoriously expanding.

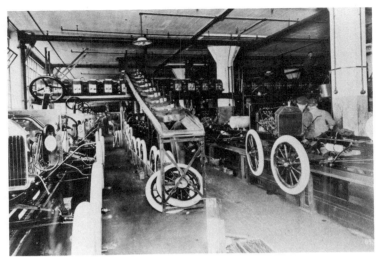

MODEL T ASSEMBLY LINES, HIGHLAND PARK PLANT, 1914
(Courtesy of FORD Motor Co., Dearborn, Michigan)

EARLY GERMAN ALBATROSS PHOTOGRAPHED LOOKING UP
THE TOWER OF A RUINED CHURCH, WORLD WAR I
(Photo courtesy of U.S. Air Force)

Artists and architects combined in militant groups, such as the Werkbund, and later De Stijl and the Bauhaus, to woo manufacturers and industrialists. They composed strident manifestos, in which the rationality of the machine was lauded as the new vision and redeeming virtue of a new century, which, following the First World War, did not seem to have much else to redeem it. Their cause took on the fervor of a crusade. Industrial towns and factories of the future were designed by Gropius, Saint Elia, Le Corbusier with the same fervor and all embracing faith, high purpose, and passion which Alberti and the early humanists felt for the form of an ideal church.

The guidelines proclaimed were gleaming hard surfaces, white electric light, elimination of ornament, repetitive form, the expression of materials, and forms that followed the function of machines. In short the artists and architects stridently proclaimed as virtue all that craftsmen previously considered plain, mean, and ordinary.

Marinetti, the futurist, in some of the most colorful industrial public relations copywriting of the time proclaimed:

...sing of the nocturnal vibrations of arsenals and workshops beneath their violent electric moons...of adventurous steamers scenting the horizon; of broad-chested locomotives prancing on the rails, like huge steel horses bridled with long tubes; and the gliding flight of aeroplanes, the sound of their propellers like the flapping of flags and the applause of an enthusiastic crowd.[3]

Theo Van Doesburg, in a more sober intellectual tone wrote:

The new spiritual artistic sensibility of the twentieth century has not only felt the beauty of the machine, but has also taken cognizance of its unlimited expressive possibilities for the arts.[4]

Artists even found inspiration in time and motion studies. Frank B. Gilbreth, an industrial engineer, and his wife the psychologist, Lillian, developed methods to visually depict and measure work movement with the objective of eliminating unnecessary motion and thus render the performance of work tasks more profitable and efficient.

The Gilbreth's scientific experiments, which reduced human action to machine action and the analysis of movement as an artistic problem in easel painting, occurred simultaneously. We find the Italian Futurists representing movement in successive phases; Carlo Carra, with his Rattling Taxi, Giacoma Bella with his Dog On The Leash, and, of course, the work that is probably the best remembered, Marcel Duchamp's Nude Descending The Staircase were all painted during the period that Gilbreth was fixing lights to workers' extremities and photographing their movements. A new artistic form representing the previously unrepresentable movement in its various phases emerged in the art gallery at the same time its results were being incorporated on the assembly line.[5]

However, this phase was short lived. By the midpoint of the second decade of the twentieth century, motion analysis was discontinued in the work place--a victim of its own success. The tasks of the assembly line worker had been successfully reduced to a few endlessly repeated manipulations.

One auto frame manufacturer summed up the situation in these words:

> *It is highly probable that watching our workers do the same thing over and over again, day in and day out, sent us on our quest for the 100% mechanization of frame manufacture. The best course seemed to eliminate him.*[6]

At this stage of art and industrial development the worker was of little interest to either the artist or the manufacturer. The Cubists and Futurists moved on to other enthusiasms shortly thereafter. Not the least of these, for the Italian Futurists, was the exploration of the mechanical wonder and machine logic involved in the First World War.

However, despite these promising artistic beginnings and the eventual victory of "Modern Art," history did not repeat itself. Brilliant effort, boundless enthusiasm, countless pronouncements, and a plethora of little magazines did not convince the industrialists and manufacturers (who were the objects of the peons of praise and for whom the new aesthetic identity had been fabricated) to adopt it. They ignored it. They much preferred their comfortable, overstuffed, knick-knack filled drawing rooms to the hard, white, gleaming surfaces, the blinding light from bare light bulbs, and sharp-cornered furniture provided them by modern designers.

Le Corbusier lamented:

One can see the same businessmen, bankers, and merchants, away from their businesses in their homes, where everything seems to contradict their real existence--rooms too small, a conglomeration of useless and disparate objects, and a sickening spirit reigning over so many shams....style of all sorts and absurd bric-a-brac. Our industrial friends seem sheepish and shrivelled like tigers in a cage; it is very clear that they are happier at their factories or in their banks.[7]

With the failure of an industrial alliance and with the growing affluence and influence of "mass man" and increasing public subsidy of the lower economic stratas, architects during the past two decades have turned their attention to "design for the people." But they find themselves now encumbered with an even more difficult heritage. The objectives and prejudices of modern architecture are entwined with those of modern art, which has not only been traditionally unpopular, but has sought to make itself anti-popular in absolute contempt of "the people" it now seeks as clients.

Ortega y Gassett spoke eloquently to this point.[8] Modern art as a whole will always have the masses against it, he claimed. Its works invariably produce a curious effect on the general public by dividing them into two groups--one a very small one, which is composed of those favorably inclined, and the other, the majority which react with hostility. Modern art has thus functioned as a social agent that segregates two different castes of men.

Ortega, in analyzing the differentiating principle that created these two antagonistic groups, conceded that all works of art arouse differences of opinion. Some observers are bound to be favorably impressed and others not. But these differences are not organic, nor are they a matter of principle. However, in the case of "the new art," and one must remember that Ortega was writing forty years ago, an innate antagonism of major consequence occurs that was much greater in intensity and different in kind than the former difference of personal taste.

It is not that the majority of people do not like the new art and the minority like it, for in the past, new ideas, if disliked, were disliked precisely because they were understood and the observer disagreed with them. But the characteristic of the new art was that it divided the public into two classes--one very small that understood and the other, the majority, that did not. The

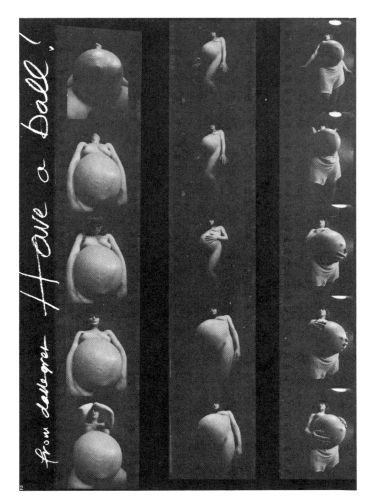

Have a ball!

from dellagren

implication was that one group possessed an organ of comprehension denied the other and, therefore, was a different variety of the human species. The new art addressed itself to a specific "gifted minority."

When a person dislikes a work of art, that they comprehend they feel superior. There is no reason for indignation. But when the dislike is due to a failure to understand, there is a feeling of vague humiliation and a sense of inferiority which is often counterbalanced by indignant self-assertion. Through its very presence, the new art compelled the average citizen to realize, in Ortega's view, that he is labeled just that--the average citizen, a creature incapable of receiving the sacrament of art, one blind, deaf, and dumb in the presence of pure beauty. The new art was a means, in Ortega's interpretation, for the elite to recognize themselves and each other in the drab mass of society and to learn their mission, which is to be few and hold their own against the many.

Today the architect and planner who attempt to work with people in the inner city are met with suspicion. The modern architects revolt against traditional values and the abandoning of former building skills in favor of art and academicism has been costly. The art of building has been left in the hands of laborers and assemblers who, to retain their dignity, develop a cynical amusement at the theorist designer's lack of technical building knowledge and a contempt for his or her supposed creative genius.

The men who wear hard hats on the job may feel envy for the designer's social position, but the prevailing attitude at the work site is one of amused contempt. The artist and architects have remained class bound, unable by education and background to understand and bridge the gap. Designers have very little exposure to comprehension, understanding, or sympathy with the conditions of building work.

But this is also due to the continuation of an older historic condition. It was proposed by manufacturers of the eighteenth and nineteenth centuries that the working classes must be saved from themselves and that their salvation lay in working long hours to restrain themselves from their proclivity for prostitution, drunkenness, and thievery. Even master craftsmen did not escape this stigma. When the Boston master joiners went on strike in 1825 for shorter hours they were opposed by the argument in the Boston papers:

...too many temptations and improvident practices from which they were happily secure when working from sunrise to sunset. It was feared and dreaded the consequence of such a measure (shorter hours) upon the morals and well-being of society.

RIOT ON 42ND STREET NEAR BROADWAY 1889. Streetcar operators went on strike in 1889. The basic issue was recognition of the workmen's organization as well as wages and hours. (From NEW YORK IN THE NINETEENTH CENTURY, Dover Books)

Similar arguments were heard in all industrial countries and were invariably brought to bear when demands for shorter hours arose. Yet, in violent contrast to this attitude on the part of their employers, the major struggles of working men, women, and children during the nineteenth century were directed toward shorter working days, which took precedence over all other demands, including pay and safety, both of which were equally mean and cruel. If the claims of mill owners and industrialists were correct, then the bloody strikes for the eight-hour work day were undoubtedly the most concerted campaigns in history in favor of lewdness, thievery, and debauchery.

However, during these years of fierce struggle as the ten-hour day replaced the twelve and the eight replaced the ten, crime, prostitution, and debauchery did not increase. Instead, the incidence of tuberculosis and child mortality was reduced and public schools were founded first by the workmen themselves at their own expense and later by local governments.

It is understandable that the nineteenth-century manufacturers, who bought labor, and, the workmen, who sold it, should view leisure time differently. The former saw it as lost profit and the latter as an extension of their life potential. However, when a century after the strike of the Boston joiners we find the most eminent and enlightened of modern architects, Le Corbusier, mouthing the work prejudices of an eighteenth- and nineteenth-century industrialist, there can be little wonder that the philosophy of modern art is suspect among working people.

As you will recall Le Corbusier had this to say:

The eight hour day! The three "eights" in the factory! The shifts working in relays...you will say...the worker is sufficiently cultivated to know how to make a healthy use of so many hours of liberty. But this is exactly not the case...his mind [is] not sufficiently educated to use all these hours of liberty.[9]

In conclusion and synopsis we know that modern architects attempted to repeat history, using machine forms in place of the pagan forms of antiquity, as Renaissance artists had done before them. Their purpose was to establish a rational world based on the beneficial uses of industry and manufacture, as well as to establish their status as spokesmen for an estab-

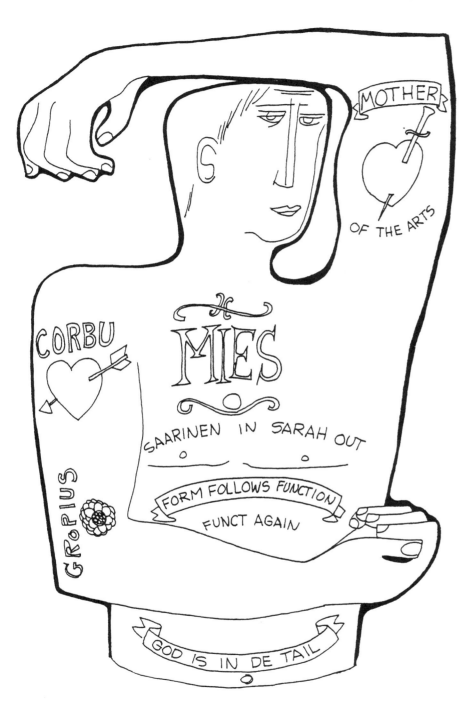

lished industrial class. Yet their overtures were rejected. The men of taste did not become men of power, as did their Renaissance predecessors. We then find the emergence of such manifestos as Le Corbusier's Architecture or Revolution, Adolph Loose's Decoration and Crime, and Neutra's Survival Through Design.

These works and ideas were far from scholarly or theoretical cultural comments. They were little more than strident threats and warnings, petulant scare tactics in a campaign to establish an artistic mysticism and cruciality. They did little more than confirm the wisdom of consigning architects to a clown society.

The combination of social situation, particularly nature of country, people, and historical tradition that occurred in Tuscany, five centuries earlier, did not materialize. Instead of entrance into the privileged class, designers today are most often associated with the antics of the Jacurilla Apache's black and white striped shaman.

It is not suggested here in this slightly exaggerated and slightly satirical capsulation of history that designers were or are evil men. They were and usually are men and women of high ideals and great talent, who have given the world many amazing architectural curiosities. The artists of, what we loosely term, the "modern movement" were men superbly trained as artists, but poorly educated in the ways of work. They were learned, rather than learning, men, who were forced to use arrogance as a public relations device. When the society did not conform to their learned conclusions, they became petulant, rather than searchers for ways to be useful.

footnotes

1. Nikolaus Pevsner – AN OUTLINE OF EUROPEAN ARCHITECTURE, Pelican, Baltimore, Md., 1943 (pp. 174–177).
2. Joseph Campbell – THE MASKS OF GOD, Primitive Methodology, Viking Press, N.J., 1956 (p. 73).
3. Paul Overy – DE STIJL, Studio Vista, London, 1969 (p. 33).
4. Charles Jencks – MODERN MOVEMENTS IN ARCHITECTURE, Doubleday Anchor, N.Y.C., 1973 (p. 33).
5. Siegfried Giedeion – MECHANIZATION TAKES COMMAND, The Norton Library, N.Y.C., 1948 (p. 103).
6. Ibid., (p. 118).
7. Le Corbusier – TOWARDS A NEW ARCHITECTURE, Praeger, N.Y.C., 1960.
8. Ortega y Gasset – THE DEHUMANIZATION OF ART, Anchor Books, Garden City, N.Y., 1948 (pp. 5–7).
9. Le Corbusier – TOWARDS A NEW ARCHITECTURE, (p. 255).

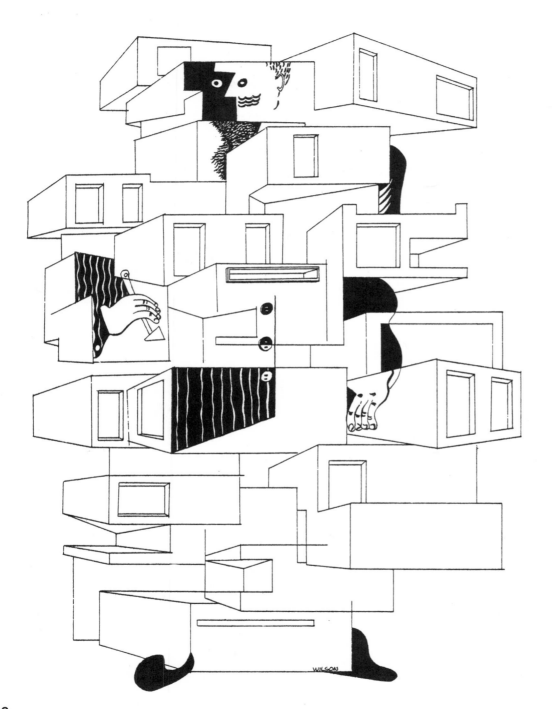

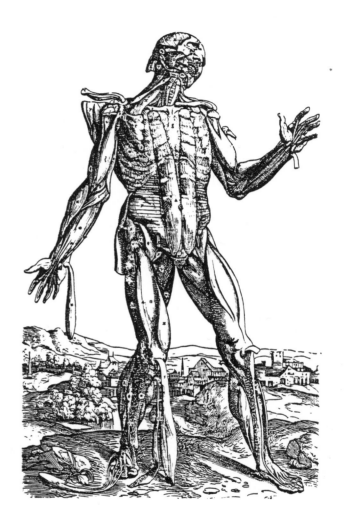

THE FIFTH PLATE OF THE MUSCLES
BY ANDREAS VESALIUS, CIRCA 1540

The Architectural Placebo

The psychoanalyst Laing is convinced that Western man is mad. Erich Fromm spoke of our dark period of insanity. The notion that the world and its institutions have gone awry is not restricted to the critics of the mind. Ada Louise Huxtable, the architectural critic for the New York Times, wrote on March 15, 1970 that one practical decision after another has led to the brink of cosmic disaster and "there we sit, in pollution and chaos, courting the end of the earth." Wolf Von Eckardt, architectural critic for the Washington Post, wrote in the August 6, 1977 issue of the New Republic:

> *As the architecture conceived by Walter Gropius at the Bauhaus in Weimer and by Le Corbusier in his atelier in Paris...had long been feverish, erractic, and contradictory. There had been a lot of doctoring. But no one got at the basic affliction which was that Modern Architecture is an abstract art--an abstraction that failed to meet practical human needs.*

There seems little question in critical minds that we and our institutions are a bit feverish and fay. One of the more demonstrable truths of this diagnosis is that architecture, as an unpredictable "mother" of the arts, has turned to faith healing and placebos to cure the ills of the built environment. We find architects employing remedies very much akin to the sixteenth-and seventeenth-century powders of sympathy.

Sir Kenelm Digby's (1603-65) "sympathetic powder" was a revival and improvement of an earlier cure called "weapon ointment." Weapon ointment was applied to the weapon that inflicted the wound, while the wound itself was left unattended. Weapon liniment was concocted from ingredients that appealed strongly to the imagination, such as eunuch's fat or moss from a criminal's skull. Cotton Mather used crushed sow bugs, body lice, and incinerated toads in his practice, and in the late Middle Ages the apothecaries of Europe complained bitterly that the crocodile dung they imported from Egypt was shamefully adulterated by dishonest traders. These substances were administered to the wounds of common soldiers because they were cheaper than mummies, unicorn's horns, bezoar stones, pearls, and potable gold, which were remedies prescribed for the nobility.[1]

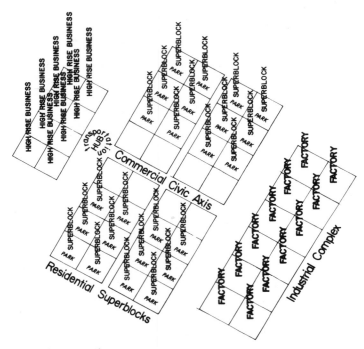

La Ville Radieuse

PLAN FOR AN IDEAL INDUSTRIAL CITY, Le Corbusier, 1927

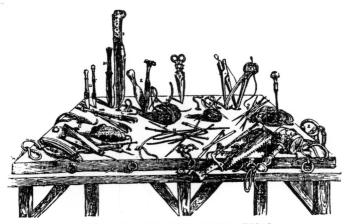

SIXTEENTH CENTURY SURGICAL TOOLS

Given such remedies, Sir Digby's sympathetic powder was an inspired stroke of genius. It was applied to the blood-stained clothing surrounding the wound. This constituted a much more effective remedy, since the weapon that inflicted the wound was an accessory often difficult to obtain without incurring more wounds.

Sympathetic powder is not much different in concept than the coordination of "street furniture" and the application of art to architecture in bankrupt New York City or, for that matter, than the awarding of a commission to beautify Lenox Avenue after the Harlem riots to three of the nation's most prestigious architects.

Sympathetic powder was an effective remedy. A wound that had been washed, bandaged, and left to heal was less prone to infection than one ever so carefully anointed with either genuine or counterfeit crocodile dung. It was undoubtedly less harmful to commission the beautification of Lenox Avenue than it would have been to assign these three architects the task of cauterizing the slums on either side of it with "significant forms."

During the time that Ambroise Pare (1510-90), the great French physician, studied surgery on the battlefields of France, the cautery was the accepted medical treatment used to stop hemorrhage. Boiling oil, molten pitch, or a red-hot iron was applied to the bleeding surface. The pain was agonizing and the wound healed slowly as a result of the additional injury. Pare cleaned the wound and tied the ends of blood vessels as surgeons do today.[2] But Pare was the rare exception among sixteenth century healers and not the rule. Given the general practices of sixteenth- and seventeenth-century medicine, the placebo of Sir Digby's sympathetic powder was a medical breakthrough as startling as transplanting a baboon's heart to a human chest seems today.

Today's architectural practice, when viewed objectively, will show that much of the good performed by the profession occurs precisely because architects no longer apply the equivalent of boiling pitch and red-hot irons to the wounds of the built environment. The use of artistic sympathetic powders, which provide rare and precious materials for the wealthy and common onces for the poor, has a beneficial effect upon the most grievous environmental illness of our time, precisely because architects have found themselves unable to cauterize urban illness with their radiant cities, meaningful spaces, articulated forms, and prescriptions.

PALACE OF THE DAWN, BRAZILIA, OSCAR NEIMEYER, ARCHITECT
(Courtesy of George Braziller, New York)

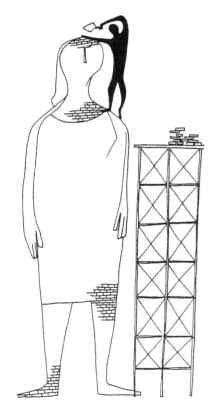

ARCHITECTS MAKE BETTER PEOPLE
(Architect making friend)

The absolute verifiable environmental knowledge that the architectural profession can bring to bear upon building problems is derived from its studies of aesthetics, and is no less exact in many ways than that possessed by the barbers and hog gelders who composed the predominant segment of the medical profession in Digby's time.

Almost two decades ago, Sir Herbert Read, the Pare of art history, posed the problems of modern architecture in his book Art and Industry. Read diagnosed the urgent problem of the time as the transformation of a million slum dwellings into cities of order, light, health, and convenience. Although the numbers are now multimillions, the diagnosis remains remarkably accurate. Those engaged in the practical problems of transformation will find questions of ornament and decoration singularly futile and academic--a waste of time and money. The problem is not academic, but rational and human, Read contended.

Housing that will embody an ideal of decent living on a communal scale can only be designed and built with imagination and science. But what more has any great work of art ever required? In the solution of this immediate practical problem of our day, all the necessary opportunities for a great tradition of design exist. If the tradition is not realized, if this opportunity is not seized, Read thought, it will be due to the imposition of false and irrelevant ideas of art.

Doctors, for all of their virtuosity, scientific and medical technology, cannot build a new human being any more than the art of architecture can renew and restore health to urban areas, no matter how ingenious the design nor how great its artistic merit. The doctor's best efforts are simply directed toward finding ways of helping the body regain its balance as a means for the body to heal itself. The architect can do no more; yet this is a truth that architects, with their faith in the mysterious power of good design, find it hard to realize. The contention of Winston Churchill that first we form our buildings and then our buildings form us is the basis of this architectural fallacy. People can make love in a refrigerator; it simply is not much of an aid to the activity. Architects can help people realize their aspirations, but no building, no matter how well designed, can give meaning to a life that does not already possess a purpose. During the wars of the Renaissance, soldiers occasionally stabled their horses in cathedrals, and there is no record that it had any effect on either the soldiers or the horses.

AUTOMOTIVE ENGINE GUIDED INTO BODY POSITION AS
ASSEMBLY LINE MOVES AT THIRTY FEET PER SECOND
(Courtesy of General Motors Corporation)

Read blamed the concoction of aesthetic sympathetic powder on the academies, institutes, and schools of art. This includes schools of architecture, for despite the architects dalliance in the sciences, schools of architecture remain dominated by the aesthetic objectives of the design studio. Read claimed that we would benefit from the total abolition of all academic instruction in art, and that the only necessary instruction was technical, for out of technical instruction the practical question of design automatically emerges.

But if academic education is to be abolished, another form of education must be substituted, Read warned. He proposed that the general principles of harmony and proportion and the development of sensuous and intellectual perceptivity be taught on an extensive scale, like mathematics, to all school children in the junior grades.

The origins of artistic sympathy powder can be traced to the introduction of machine methods into industry. The machine is defined here as an instrument or tool of mass production. Every tool is a machine--the hammer, the axe, and the chisel, as well as power-driven machinery. The distinction is made not in the tools or industrialization, for the factory system as we will recall existed in classical Greece, but in their use. This can be measured by the ability of the tool user to exercise his or her will during the fashioning of artifacts. The Greek vases of the fifth century were used to export wine and olive oil and were found in the ruins of all the cities bordering Greek trade routes. These no-deposit/no-return containers of the classic world were remarkably beautiful and varied even though constructed on a pottery assembly line.

If the tool answers to the human will to form, then art is a normal by-product of this activity; for art, as Read contended, springs from technology. Art is nothing more than the intelligent use of tools, or, at least, this has been its definition during most of its history. Worringer tells us that there was no word for fine art among medieval builders. The artist was merely the most expert craftsman. Even in classical Greece there was only one word, tekhne for art.[3]

But the plight of the artist is the least of our worries, for the artist gains his or her status from the skillful use of tools. The poor condition of the activity that we term "fine art" is merely a symptom, not the malady itself. The

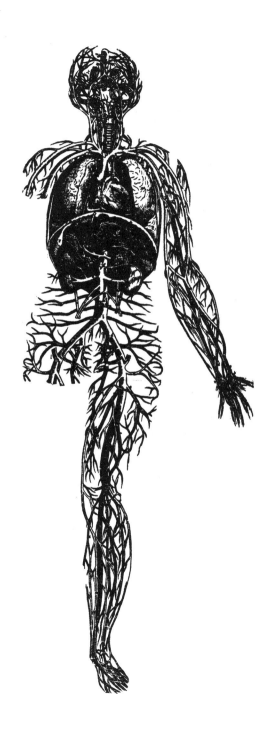

illness can be traced to the damage done to the will to form of all working, tool-using people. The pitiful state of the "precious artistic soul" of the singular artist and architect is just that-- pitiful. But humankind's deprivation of the natural satisfaction that comes from meaningful work is a horrible tragedy.

We have known what the peculiar use of tools called industrialization does to human beings in the modern world almost as long as we have lived with it. We have been warned by such men as Jefferson, de Tocqueville, Horatio Greenough, Meyhew, Alinski, and Terkel, and daily we suffer the injuries to our sensibilities. No amount of affluence, no surfeit of manufactured artifacts derived from the division of labor and industrial production can cure us. A man working on an assembly line all week is not compensated by a ride in his automobile on Sunday afternoon.

The malignant stage in the use of machine-age tools was devel- oped over the past two centuries and its beginnings coincide almost exactly with the first concoction of artistic sympathetic powder. The spinning jenny, the weaving machines, and the steam engine were invented toward the end of the eighteenth century. The revolution in practical life that followed these inventions was of an amazing historic suddenness. The rise of modern art or fine art and in- dustrial design coincides with the declining fortunes of the crafts- men and the rise of the industrial proletariet, who John Habraken has defined as those who cannot house themselves. The Luddite riots in England in 1811 and 1816 mark the acute stage of the worker's resistance to the loss of their ability to lead lives as independent craftsmen exercising their will to form over their tools. Frederick Taylor's introduction of industrial management at the Midvale Steel Plant in the latter part of the 1880s marks the triumph of mindless working tools in America.

Artistic sympathetic powder began modestly as a response to an immediate industrial problem at the beginnings of the nineteenth century. At that time, the machine seemed a monster devouring raw materials at one end and turning out finished articles at the other, while grinding out the individual worker's will to form in the process. But mass- produced industrial products did not appeal to potential purchasers accustomed to the quality and uniqueness of crafted artifacts. Industrialists, not artists, were the ones to realize that art might solve this problem. Other things being equal, they reasoned, the most "artistic" product would win the market. Art seemed to them to be the product that would sell all others.

PICTURE GALLERY FROM HARPER'S MAGAZINE, 1882

PEOPLE'S GALLERY OF ADVERTISING ART FROM HARPER'S MAGAZINE, 1882

Product sales was the idealistic motivation that prompted industrialists to introduce culture to the masses in the nineteenth century, as public relations is the reason industrialists support art today.

Sir Robert Peel, a great statesman who was also an industrial magnet, was among the first to support the establishment of a National Gallery. In a speech before the House of Commons on April 13, 1832, the issue that officially placed art in a discussion of economic affairs was raised. Peel declared that motives of public gratification were not the only ones the House should consider in the matter of establishing a National Gallery. The interest of manufacturers was also involved in the fine arts. Peel pointed out that English machines and mechanics were far superior to all others, but that they were not as successful in the matter of designs that appealed to the tastes of the consumers. English manufacturers were, therefore, in a difficult competitive position. Elevating the common taste was of considerable commercial importance. A Lord Ashley commented during the same debate that the display of works of science and art, such as the calculating machine of Mr. Babbage, had collateral advantages, since improvements in machinery had occurred in Glasgow as a result of the exhibition of the machine in that city. Ashley considered that the erection of a gallery would be beneficial for artists, mechanics, and the industrious classes and would be a further boon because it would keep workers out of "ale houses."

A Mr. Hume added his voice to the debate, declaring that there was only one man in Coventry who was proficient in making designs for silk and he had had to plagiarize his designs from foreigners. The concern for popular taste is as unique a virtue of industrialization as is environmental neglect and alcoholism.

The manufacturers had decided that they would buy art like any other commodity and apply it to their products. The marriage of art and industry was one of convenience. Industry gave art a home and she became a most "happy hooker," the designing woman of industrial design. The arrangement has remained a permanent one, with industry today paying greater court than ever before, although for entirely different reasons.

Herman Mathesius, who, from 1896 until 1903 was attached to the German Embassy in London for research on English housing, brought the idea back with him to Germany. In formulating the program of the "Werkbund," Mathesius declared in June, 1914:

As long as a universal high level of taste has not been achieved, we cannot count on German arts and crafts making their influence effectively felt abroad....it is a matter of life and death for Germany constantly to ennoble its production.... The existence of efficient large-scale business concerns with reliable good tasts is a pre-requisite for any export. [4]

By the time Walter Gropius had organized the Bauhaus, the collaboration of art and industry was an established artistic ideal. The Bauhaus sought to corner the market through the concept of total design, in which the architect would be responsible for all artifacts, from teapots to skyscrapers.

The concept of art as a placebo has persisted and gathered considerable momentum. In the 1950s the Museum of Modern Art in New York continued the tradition with its "Good Design" series organized and conducted in conjunction with the Chicago Merchandise Mart.

From the very beginning of industrial domination of tools, as craftsmanship, which was formerly the expression of individual will to form, was eliminated from the industrial workplace, the need for a specialized person, the designer for industry, emerged. The designer assumed the task of materializing culture in the form of manufactured products. Design, that formerly unique quality that grew from the relation of the worker to his tools and materials now became a unifying style imposed to promote product sales.

It did not take manufacturers too much longer to realize that if materializing culture would sell the product, then the important element of manufacture was style. Design became the sympathetic powder to heal the all too human desire for that unique quality of environment that makes a person's place his or her own. Styles are used to create demand, to make products obsolete, and more is spent upon them and their delivery than on the product itself.

UNLEADED

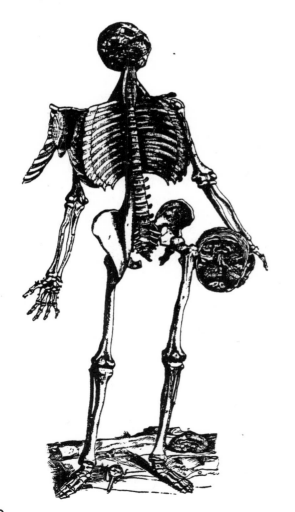

The more deprived people are of the ability to express their will to form, in leaving their mark upon their surroundings, in asserting their individuality in the face of the patterns that are imposed upon them, the more demands are made upon the designer to supply a uniqueness to satisfy this desire for individuality. Art is the sympathetic powder used to soothe the hurt of individual frustration and the desire for individual expression. But individual uniqueness is a personal attribute, and the designer can no more supply this quality to others than designers can eat, sleep, or make love in their stead.

Architects today are being treated to a dose of their own sympathetic powder by the programmer, and at last are becoming aware, as Von Eckardt observes, that their feverish activities are not a passing virus, but the symptoms of serious illness.

An interesting transformation is that aesthetic sympathetic powder has far outgrown the product. The "Business Committee for the Arts," (BCA), an Association of Major US Corporations, donates more than twice the amount of money that Congress allocates to the National Foundation for the Arts.

The artist who designs for industry is of minor importance when compared to industry's involvement in the arts as a means not of selling their products, but of selling itself to the consumer. The government encourages this by tax systems which allow tax benefits for financing the arts both in advertising budgets and company expenses.

The modest thirty thousand pounds that Sir Peel requested from the House of Commons to start a National Gallery has grown to a 221 million dollar subsidy of the arts in 1976 by major corporations. Culture is no longer a sales come-on, but a means of convincing common cultured taste that what is good for Exxon is good for America, and that is Masterpiece Theater.

In a Washington Post story of July 24, 1977, which described the Medicilike beneficence of Big Business, it was stated that, according to a recent study done for the BCA by the New York accounting firm of Touche Ross, five major oil companies donated a total of just under two million dollars to the arts in 1973--the last year of cheap gasoline and no energy worries for the American public--but gave twelve and one-half million last year, which constitutes a 540 percent increase in four years.

Vasari

ON

TECHNIQUE

LooT

THE

GOLDEN

$ECTION

*We don't know who discovered water—
but we are certain it wasn't a fish.*

Donald S. Naughton, Chairman of the Board of Prudential Insurance Corporation and a member of the Board of Directors of Exxon and AT&T, gave the main reason as, "that they don't have to advertise their gasoline. They're selling more than they want to sell, so there's a vast amount of money that can go into the performing arts. Secondly, the industry, rightly or wrongly, has a bad image, and they're using this as a means of trying to improve it."

Thomas A. Yates, Director of Communications for the William Underwood Company, stated, "Like all profit-making organizations we are interested in the bottom line. Increasing and improving our cultural surroundings is a worthwhile goal in itself, and it also has its benefit for the company. We support the arts because it's good business." Said one executive, "They don't get a lot of publicity, they buy it, and all at a superb level of taste, and all deductible."

We must not blame the corporations. They are following in a noble tradition. We know that during the latter part of the Middle Ages the custom of insinuating the portrait of the donor into works of art designed for the church emerged. In any series of works of art, say altar pieces or stained-glass windows, you will observe how, in the fourteenth and fifteenth centuries, the portrait of the donor gradually grows in size and importance, until, in the sixteenth century, the donor is painted on the same scale as the sacred figures and even comes to dominate the whole composition.[5]

The placebo of artistic sympathetic powder has persisted for so long that we have learned to accept the illness. We no longer have the cultural energy to resist Exxon.

But a cure is possible; the spirit of Pare is not dead. We can re-examine our idea of art, for the concept of architecture allied exclusively with the fine arts is as rational as returning the practice of medicine to barbers and hog gelders.

Since the human mind tends to link unrelated events and seek connections between them, we may propose an idea that is absolutely removed from the patterns of thought worn into the memory surfaces of our minds by the prejudices of fine art and thus find a remedy for our feverish and fay condition. Obviously we cannot cure the condition of architecture as we have described it. We can, however, like any good doctor, change our diagnosis.

The idea proposed is that architecture is not wholly an art or problem-solving device, as it is currently defined, but rests upon the natural outgrowth of the intelligent use of tools manifested in "the will to form" of all those who use them. If we first enlarge our definition of architecture to include the common and ordinary acts of creativity (as each coral polyp contributes its body into the coral's eventual form) which are part of all building, we may then see architecture as the sum of the countless anonymous acts of creativity of myriads of anonymous builders. Then an entirely different view of what we term architecture, the art of building, begins to emerge.

The art of architecture is then open to all comers. It is not necessary to have a degree or be certified as creative to validate building accomplishments. It is merely necessary to actually create good building, which is much easier than earning a degree.

Perhaps never before in history has there been a greater desire or more obvious manifestation of peoples' desire to divest themselves of the patterns imposed upon them. With this desire has come a great upsurge of creative means of expression, manifesting itself everywhere in the built environment. We find it from the self-built housing in the technically less-developed nations to the do-it-yourselfers in the suburbs of the highly industrialized countries. Never have so many books on how-to-do things without the help of experts been published. Never have there been so many adaptions of building forms to life-styles, from the self-contained communities of the truck stops, to the communes of city lofts. Service stations become pizza parlors and photo kiosks become small delicatessens. On the highways there are the vans of the affluent middle class youth and the new language of the CB radio. The vans are homes away from home. The CB makes the communication network of the Tower of Babel a model of lucidity. But everyone on the CB has a voice, and, with it, a great poetry of "Tijuanna Taxis," "Smokey the Bears," "Beavers," and "Louisiana Porch Monkeys" came into being. Children playing with electronic parts, which they save their dollars to buy from "Radio Shacks," contact each other halfway round the globe, and housewives check their food budgets with miniature calculators, which have the mathematical capabilities to solve the equation of relativity. Peons with transistor radios tune into satellites, and teenagers convert their automobiles for an "airfoil" look that makes them look like charging gerbils in heat. Perhaps never has there been so much creativity taking

place in the built environment as a reaction against the standardized patterns imposed upon us. The conditions that Read proclaimed as necessary for great art, science, and creativity are everywhere manifest, and an architecture is taking form without architects.

An autonomous, anonymous architecture, for this is what we are describing, has emerged. If indeed architecture is not only the fine art that we find in such feverish and fay condition, but includes all the countless creative acts of building, then our concerns over the pitiful state of the fine art of architecture and its placebos are hypocritical-- the diagnosis of Hippocratic oafs. If architecture is indeed the art of creative building, then it lies not only within the narrow province of the fine artist, but in the whole wide world. If we return to the one word for art, as the Greeks defined creativity, or the idea of only coarse and fine workmen, as the medieval masons defined it, then our laments for the state of the fine art defy common sense.

Enlarging the scope of architecture shows that architecture does not have to be a cultural placebo, nor does architecture suffer from the fatal illness diagnosed. Architecture in the largér sense is suffering a slight head cold that is giving a great number of ordinary creative people a severe pain in the arse.

Architects have the choice of pursuing the moribund aesthetics of the fine arts and their placebos, or lending their vital skills as midwives to the birth of an emerging democratic architecture.

footnotes

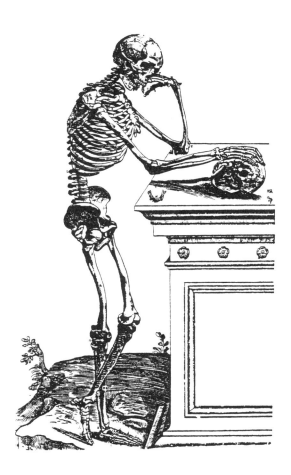

1. Howard W. Haggard, M.D. - DEVILS, DRUGS AND DOCTORS, Pocket Books Inc., N.Y.C., 1947 - Harper and Brother, N.Y.C., 1929 (pp. 343-344).
2. Ibid., (pp. 343-344).
3. Herbert Read - ART AND INDUSTRY, Indiana University Press, Bloomington, Indiana, 1961 (Read copyright 1953 - originally published in England, 1934, American edition based on 3rd revision).
4. Ulrich Conrads - PROGRAMS AND MANIFESTOES ON 20TH CENTURY ARCHITECTURE, MIT Press, Cambridge, Mass., 1970 (pp. 28-29).
5. Herbert Read - ART AND INDUSTRY, 1961 (p. 10).

Design Your Choice of Accidents

From yo-yos to skycrapers, all man-made objects are the result of some person's or some group's decision as to their use and appearance. The inescapable planned decisions of others surround, direct, aid, or hamper us in our daily lives. Accidents are the only exception. Rainwater gathering in pools on the pavement, wrecked automobiles, abandoned buildings, junk piles, and occassionally an unidentified "thing" that piques our curiosity are the only undesigned objects urban humankind ever encounters. Design is escaped only by accident.

But design itself is the major cause of accidents. Designed objects seldom remain for very long as the designer intended them to be. Useful objects are designed for a particular use, but this use is not an inherent property of their design. We find that tires are turned into toys, paper clips into tie clips, and Coke cans used as ashtrays. Whatever use the designer anticipated is invariably superceded by any number of other uses wherever this is possible. Design only remains unchanged where change is forcibly prevented.

The designer analyzes an activity and then designs an object to satisfy needs of that activity as he or she interprets it to be. The object may fulfill a great number of other needs and may even perform some of these better than it does the need for which it was originally designed.

Designs are, therefore, merely statements of the designer's opinion, based on the purpose of the object as the designer understands that purpose to be. The designer's comprehension of purpose determines how the object will look and be used. For example, the purpose of dams has always been considered by designers to be that of withstanding hydraulic pressures. If the designer's comprehension of purpose had been the redesign of water, dams would not look as they do, or perhaps would not be designed at all. We have seen the form of airplanes change drastically during the past few years, as designers have changed their idea of the uses of air, from screwing their way through it with a propeller to sucking their way through it with jets.

The form of designed things is decided by the selection of purpose and is never, as Pye stated, determined by absolute necessity. Nothing designed is the way that it is because it could be no other way.[1]

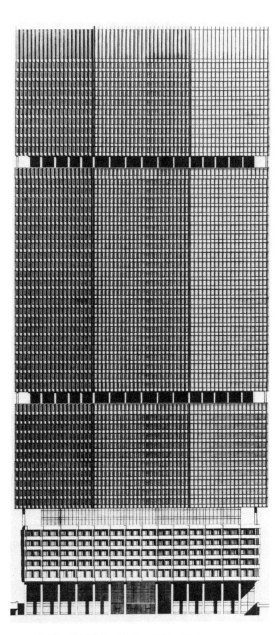

GRAND CENTRAL CITY, NEW YORK
BY THE ARCHITECTS COLLABORATIVE
(Courtesy of TAC)

JOUSTING ARMOUR, GERMAN, 1500

EIFFEL TOWER
(Courtesy of Otis
Elevator Co.)

There is another phenomenon that inevitably occurs to complicate matters further and which emphasizes the transitory nature of the designer's opinions. All designed objects inevitably involve unnecessary work, which is termed decoration, style, ornament, or embellishment. Strangely enough, as objects are used less for the purposes the designer originally intended, more of this useless work seems inevitably to be lavished upon them.

This phenomenon has occurred throughout history. We find that the body armor of fighting men reached a peak of decorative perfection in the seventeenth century, two centuries after the introduction of gunpowder had rendered armor obsolete. The joints of the armor were ingenious mechanisms that allowed great freedom of movement. Steel surfaces were covered with embossed relief, using precious metals in works of great artistic merit. Only a fool wore such armor in battle. Real fighting took place between soldiers wearing plain steel breastplates. The museums are full of such superb examples of the armorer's art, precisely because it was never worn, and thus never destroyed in battle.

On the everyday level, over the past few years, we have seen the simple punch-top can opener become increasingly decorative as it was superceded by the flip-top can and the twist-off bottle top. Punch-top can openers, which were once given away, are now elaborately decorated and sold as bar-top ornaments. They are much like the decorative souvenir teaspoons that people buy to commemorate visits to Niagara Falls or Washington D.C. These ornate utensils are proudly displayed behind glass in parlor showcases and never see the inside of a teacup.

But decorative uselessness is not confined to minor objects. Similar phenomena seem to occur in physics, religion, engineering, and economics. Sound waves become visible on the edges of an airplane's wings just as it breaks the sound barrier and sound is left behind. The great church of Saint Peter's was built in Rome on the eve of the Reformation. The Eiffel Tower, built for the 1889 Paris Exhibition, was constructed of 7,300 tons of wrought iron at the precise moment that the French had succeeded in producing the much superior building material, mild steel, in great quantities. The World Trade Center office complex was built in New York City on the eve of that metropolis' declaration of bankruptcy.

Whether useful objects are plain or decorated, they cannot help doing things that no one wants them to do. Knives get dull, airplanes fall out of the sky, and, as they increase in size, it becomes difficult to find places to put them. Automobiles smell

Costs Mount on New Opera House

Project Is Estimated at $55.3 Million— '69 Target Date

By TILLMAN DURDIN
Special to The New York Times

SYDNEY, Australia, Oct. 10 —Costs and controversy mount as construction progresses on the spectacular new opera house being built on Bennelong Point in Sydney Harbor.

SYDNEY OPERA HOUSE
(Courtesy Australian
Information Service)

LISTER BUILDING, HOUSTON, TEXAS
(Courtesy of C-E Glass
Division, Combustion Eng., Inc.)

badly, are hard to fix, wear out quickly, and are often very dangerous. Nothing seems to work as intended. David Pye thinks the reason we decorate objects so profusely is to say that if we cannot make them work, we can at least make them look presentable.

Everything designed and built has countless limitations and never exactly fits its purpose. From skyscrapers to teacups, everything proves to be an inept improvisation. Entirely satisfactory performance is never attained. On the other hand, in contrast to their intended uses, designed things are often employed for more beneficial tasks than those for which the designer originally conceived them. We find the use of the walls of the Roman Collosseum at Arles entirely reversed. Originally designed to contain cruel gladiatorial games, they were also used during the Middle Ages to protect the people within them against the barbarians outside.

Design cannot help but cause change, and change invariably occurs in a number of things. This does not imply anything planned or systematic, but only that change inevitably occurs. A smashed automobile is as much the result of design as is a perfectly functioning Swiss watch.

The designer selects a purpose in good faith and assumes that beneficial change will result from his or her design efforts. Yet the designer cannot entirely control the change that takes place and can only attempt to regulate the amount of change necessary to accomplish the purpose he or she comprehends the purpose to be. The design may, and often does, trigger unforeseen results. The one result the designer hopes to achieve does not exclude others. There are simply too many conditions impossible to control. Design can, therefore, become a very expensive activity for a very large number of people who do not enjoy its benefits, yet suffer its consequences. There are countless examples of this phenomenon all around us.

The reflective glass, so often used to control the interior temperature of buildings by reducing the penetration of solar rays, cools the building's occupants. But the reflected rays are diverted to neighboring buildings and pour down upon the heads of pedestrians in the streets below. Much of the discomfort and conflict in our urban society, noise, pollution, strip mining, highway congestion, crowding, and iotrogenic disease involve the unwanted effects of design suffered by those wo do not enjoy its benefits.

QUEEN ELIZABETH II OFFICIALLY OPENED THE SYDNEY OPERA
HOUSE ON OCTOBER 20, 1973 - REPORTED COST 100,000,000
AUSTRALIAN POUNDS (Courtesy of the Australian
Information Service)

SCHOOL CORRIDOR, NEW HAVEN GRAMMAR SCHOOL

Designed things simply function unpredictably, involve
useless work, and unwittingly become part of systems of
change that the designer cannot foresee or control. Designers
cannot be blamed for this, but we can be amazed at the absolute
assurance with which designers undertake their tasks.

The designer begins with a clearly defined intention, explicit
purpose, and a precise idea of the use to which the design will be
put. Materials are then engineered precisely as designers indicate
in specifications and drawings. Certainty of purpose and material
is the essential characteristic of manufacture and design in our
industrial society. Certainty of purpose determines the mental
climate in which the act of design takes place and is the controlling factor that determines the form of the physical environment
that results.

The so-called "international style" should not be attributed to
the inventive genius of modern architects. It was simply the only
possible architectural solution to punch-press metal products, extrusions, modular materials, and a building process organized by industrial management. Such overwhelming certainty of intent, purpose,
and product was achieved by eliminating all design decisions in the
work place. The building products that resulted are as characteristic of industrial management as are the fragmentation and standardization of work operations on the assembly line of industrial production.

The industrial imperatives that determine the form of
our built environment and direct our design processes are
accepted without question on the one hand, and we ignore the
transitory accidental nature of design on the other. We never
question the possibility that any other design method exists.
We assume that all design, throughout human history, follows
this pattern under all creative conditions, from NASA's rocket
designer to the cave painter of Altemira.

But in our haste and enthusiasm to impose a rational order,
we have overlooked the fact that industrial design is a very
recent and specialized development, unique only in its overwhelming application. An entirely different principle of
design has always coexisted, even during such monumental
planning as that which took place during the building of the
pyramids. This is a universal design principle taken for
granted outside the highly industrial nations, but can even
be found there as the common characteristic of the design
methods employed by the suburban housewife, the home craftsman,
and all people unschooled in design who change the world
around them.

WINDOW DETAIL, SAN CRISTOBAL, MEXICO
(Courtesy of John Sheperd)

This is a principle of design almost opposite in every respect to that of industrial design. It begins with no preconceived idea, and properties of materials are sensed rather than known. Material, purpose, and use all fuse into one spontaneous realization. Consistency of result is impossible to achieve, for the creator uses his or her intelligence during all aspects of the work and is free to explore all possibilities inherent in the materials and purpose as they occur to them.

We can see the evidences in the work of hand weavers who always bring individuality to their craft. Artists very seldom work with preconceived notions. American carpenters from Colonial times until well into this century always added unique twists and turns and decoration to their work. Where their buildings have survived, they are as unique as those of any architect's today. The craftsmen always seek to give a little bit more of themselves, a bit more than asked of them. In contrast, industrially managed labor is consistently standardized and reduced with respect to quality of workmanship and materials.

The opposing design principle, which we will term "spontaneous design," in direct contrast to industrial design, assumes that the instant the object is conceived to be useful, the idea of purpose originates. The need, the object's possible usefulness, the properties of the material are all secondary to this spontaneous realization. No preconceptions exist. The designer's mind is open to all possibilities. If, in fashioning, the idea goes wrong, then there is always the possibility of diverting the object to some other use, which may suggest itself.

In contrast to industrial design, which imposes extreme limitations on variety, invention, and inspiration of means and materials, intuitive or suggestive design is never twice the same. Design theories are therefore of little consequence.

When a person picks up a log on the beach or finds a discarded or junked object that suggests use as a column or lintel in the house he or she is building and applies it for that purpose, it may be many times as strong as it would have been had it been designed and calculated for either of these purposes. In fact, the entire structure, if built in this manner, will be redundant in bracing and shoring. The problem of structural stability does not, therefore, require advanced calculation or planning.

FAVELA, SQUATTER HOUSING ON HILLSIDE
SANTA TEREZA, CATUMBI, BRAZIL

CONTUNTO HABITACIONAL DO GABINAL, GOVERNMENT
HOUSING FOR SQUATTERS, JACAREPANGUA, BRAZIL

Christopher Alexander once contrasted what he termed the "unself-conscious" and the "self-conscious" process of adaption, which serves as an excellent description of the differences between the conditions of spontaneous and industrial design.

In the unself-conscious process the owner makes the dwelling and lives in it. There is a special closeness of contact between human and building which results in constant rearrangement and improvement of any unsatisfactory detail. The builder responsible for the original shaping of the form is aware of its demands. Anything that needs to be changed is adjusted at once.

Tent dwellers dig a trench to carry off the rain if the water threatens to seep underneath its edges. The Eskimo reacts constantly to every change in temperature inside the igloo he has built by opening holes or closing them with lumps of snow. The inhabitant realizes that something must be done about a building problem and simply does it. The failure or inadequacy of the form leads directly to its correction. The basic principle of adaption provides an incentive to change. Good fit requires no action. The process eventually reaches the equilibrium of well-fitting form. The possibilities of change, of adaption, of intelligent use of materials under these circumstances are as unlimited as humankind's creative ability.

In contrast, Alexander described what he terms the "self-conscious" process, in which reaction to failure becomes less and less direct. Materials are no longer close at hand. Buildings are more permanent, frequent repair and adjustment is less common. Construction is no longer in the hands of those that live in the building. Failures have to be reported several times and described in great detail before the specialist who will attend to them can recognize failures and make some adjustment. Response is such that problems must be of considerable magnitude before they induce correction.

Surveys and user-need studies are done to take the place of the spontaneous adaption of individuals to their dwellings. Surfaces are hard and unyielding, easily cleaned to resist the marks of user occupancy. Choice, change, ambiguity, are eliminated from the design solution. Maintenance data is programmed into the solution and design is used as an aggressive agent of suppressing human imprint.

The principles of industrial design are useful in the design of public buildings, bridges, highways, and large

MARINE MIDLAND PLAZA, LOWER BROADWAY, NEW YORK CITY
(Photos by F. Wilson)

FREE ENTERPRISE DECLARATION, MERIDA, MEXICO
(Courtesy of John Sheperd)

impersonal structures which are determined by the community. The conflict occurs when the same principles of design that built the World Trade Center are applied to all design conditions large and small.

The principle of industrial design is universally applied as the only recognized design principle. Spontaneous design is confined to the narrow range of personal choice which people can discover in the interstices between planned design systems.

The only resource left for the unsuppressible impulse of chance design lies in materials and objects that were once designed for a specific purpose and that have been discarded, have become obsolete, or have been rendered useless by accident. The great treasure house of spontaneous design, submerged but unsuppressed, are junk heaps and the abandoned and discarded artifacts of industrial production.

When design is determined by spontaneous realization using materials of unknown properties, structures are invariably over designed for their purpose. They will stand and serve the use originally conceived, but can also be altered to serve a number of other purposes. Choice remains a continuous possibility.

Spontaneous design is a universal phenomenon occurring wherever people and materials come together without interference. This universal will to form is the common denominator found in the affluent suburbs of the industrialized nations, the scavenger house of the "counterculture," the Barriadas of Mexico and South America, and the "Shanty Towns" that have sprung up all over the world.

Spontaneous design creates value from purpose. A piece of junk becomes valuable and valuable artifacts may prove ·useless. A house may become a church, a beer can a lamp. The unruly ox is converted to usefulness in the stew pot. The tree that fails to bear fruit becomes firewood, abandoned service stations become pizza parlors, and drain culverts can become houses in a cycle of constant use and adaption.

The fault of industrial design is not in intention, but in its suppression of the enormous variety of actual means employed in the social mechanism of production and change, which must be suppressed to realize the principles of optimization. It is this attitude of single-minded efficiency that dictates that the minimum amount of resources in labor and materials be expended to achieve a single result.

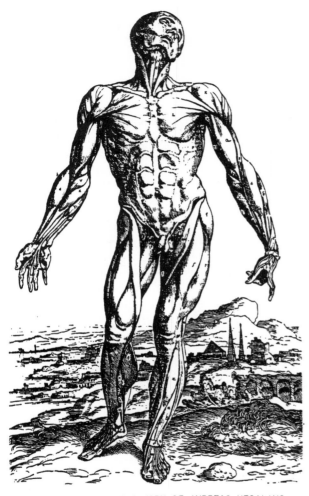

ILLUSTRATION FROM THE WORK OF ANDREAS VESALIUS

A properly designed structure will have only that degree of redundancy, known as a "safety factor," that will be sufficient to render the structure functional in the presence of the uncertainties involved in the calculation of stresses associated with its use. All other possibilities are thus eliminated. The system is wasteful because it willfully ignores the accidental nature of design and restricts use to a very narrow range of possibilities.

In reality, to design is to encourage accidents. We know that despite preconceptions, planning, and stringent control, design remains as Pye described it, imperfect and unpredictable, evolved from an analysis of use determined by the designer's narrow concept of purpose. Design involves change, but change cannot be controlled. The most the designer hopes to achieve is a change that is more beneficial than the unpredictable change that invariably occurs. The industrial designer designs with absolute faith in this accident-prone process. The designer's feet are firmly planted in the quicksand of unpredictability.

The research undertaken by an industrial designer prior to beginning a design can be compared to the study of animal behavior, for it dissects the problem in much the same way as we use vivisection on animals. We learn about a dog's paw, its leg, its viscera, its vocal cords, and its ears, but we cannot determine what makes the dog bark. When reassembled the dog has lost the capacity. We have learned something about dead dogs, but not very much about live ones. The design analysis of industrial design may have important uses in some instances, but is not of much help in creating a living environment.

We might consider the case of Ivan Petrovich Pavlov, the great Russian psychologist and experimental psychologist who discovered the mechanisms of conditioned reflex. Pavlov repeatedly rang a bell and simultaneously fed a dog. He discovered that the dog salivated when the bell was rung, whether fed or not. For years it was assumed from this experiment, that there was a connection between the sound of the bell and salivation. It was also assumed that this was significant in understanding dog and human nature, and theories of behavior for both dogs and humans were predicated upon this premise. However, recent research established the fact that the dog would have salivated as a result of Pavlov's physical action, whether the bell was rung or not. The bell was unnecessary. The bell was for Pavlov, who had interpreted an accident as purpose.

APARTMENT HOUSE FACADE, NEW YORK CITY
(Photo by F. Wilson)

Designers, from researches such as these, have become experts like Evel Knievel. They are spectacular at hurdling twenty school buses, but our blood runs cold when we think of them at the wheel of a school bus full of children.

In the controlled, unpredictable world of planned and built form, spontaneous design is user self-defense, a means of asserting the primacy of human uniqueness, of turning accident to benefit. Readaption of artifacts is the sole remaining defense left to the prisoners of industrial design and its unpredictable consequences.

Shanty towns, home craftsmen, do-it-yourselfers, suburban remodelers, the reuse of junked and wrecked artifacts are creative outlets for the fenced in, captive public that suffers the unwanted effects of design. It is the means for asserting the primacy of personal myth, for gaining a home from an economic system that denies that right, for circumventing banks and professional services that no longer serve their purpose. It is a reaction against the overwhelming design patterns that have eliminated impulse, surprise, ingenuity, and curiosity from our urban world.

Vandalism becomes a means of self-defense, ugliness a means of self-assertion defended with fierce pride. The statement, "I don't know anything about art, but I know what I like," is not necessarily the statement of a cultural "know nothing." It may well be the assertion of a person who knows too much.

footnotes

1. David Pye - THE NATURE OF DESIGN, Reinhold, N.Y.C., 1974.

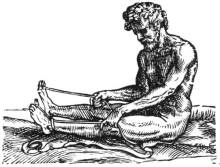

person   architect   *a pink flamingo*

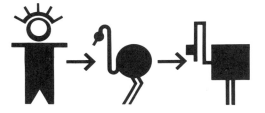

the flamingo as significant form

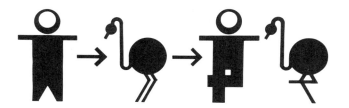

a flamingo fandango

Another View of Good Design--
with a defense of pink flamingoes

Thus far we have spoken of the nature of modern work and how it has been forcibly divided into intelligence and action, design and drudgery. This division is not the inevitable outcome of industrialization, but the result of the peculiar organization of work that took place during the latter part of the nineteenth century.

All technology followed the work patterns set at that time and now reinforces the dichotomy of hand and brain in the work place. The introduction of systems analysis after World War II and the methodologies that emerged with the computer continue to reinforce and widen the division between those who work mindlessly and those who make decisions for them.

The professions that emerged to manage a mindless work force consciously seek to benefit from this division of work. Their importance increased in direct ratio to the degree of repetitious and meaningless action performed in the work place. The design professions have been essential to the development of industrialization until the introduction of automation. Now they are obsolete. Crucial decisions are made by programmers who program designers.

The inbred arrogance of the design professions, sharpened by their association with the modern movement in art which purposely sought to make itself antipopular, prevents designers from understanding the living conditions of ordinary people, whose need for housing is the major architectural challenge of our time.

Designers persistently cling to the image of themselves as fine artists even though the function of the "fine arts" has been denigrated to that of advertising medium for major business institutions. Industrial design, and all design is industrial design in a society dominated by industrialization, has become irrational, ludicrous, and accident prone. But we may look to other design methods, almost forgotten, that have served ordinary people well from the beginning of history and that continue to be used as the core of their creativity. We will find in them the beginnings of a revitalization of the activity of design. But to do so we must understand that design is only one aspect of work.

115

WATER WHEEL, LOVE, VIRGINIA
(Photo by John Sheperd)

Every form of production engenders patterns of design and work relationships that dominate its organization and its thinking, yet within itself contains the seeds of change. In the final section of this book we will examine the sprouting of these seeds which, during the past two decades, have grown into healthy, although fragile, plants. They are now forcing themselves between the interstices of what once seemed a monolithic, mindless, indifferent bastion and their roots crack its stones.

A shift of vision is necessary to distinguish the vital growths in our industrial society from the rotting rocks that surround them. The shift of vision is an optical illusion in which a contradiction occurs between the visual facts read by the eye and the brains interpretation. Reality is organized in a different framework and appears in new perspective. A shift in the reality of the design professions is taking place. The picture is so large that it cannot be seen in its entirety, yet the outlines of another view that places humankind, instead of its products, at the center is discernible. As we become more accustomed to the characteristics of the new growth, more examples reveal themselves.

We can focus on ideas that promote the sharing of the intelligence of work with those who desire to use their energy instead of their purchasing power, who seek some of the joy of building and see the triumph of the chick in the egg, instead of the technology of the eggbeater.

What follows is not an attempt to predict the future growth of these ideas which are unpredictable. For it may be possible, as Edward De Bono pointed out, to anticipate the path of a bicycle with either an elliptical, square, or triangular front wheel, using some mathematics and what we know of physical laws. But when the cyclist chooses to ride only on the rear wheel, forecasts are useless. History is full of people "popping wheelies" on predictions.[1]

This is not an attempt to introduce new ideas or new research. The essential facts have not changed, only their interpretations. Not too long ago walls were placed around cities to keep wild things out. Today we build walls around wild things to keep people out. The meaning of boundary has changed. Architects formerly designed only very special buildings and ordinary people built for themselves. Today almost all buildings are built by specialists and very few people build for themselves. The meaning of architecture has changed.

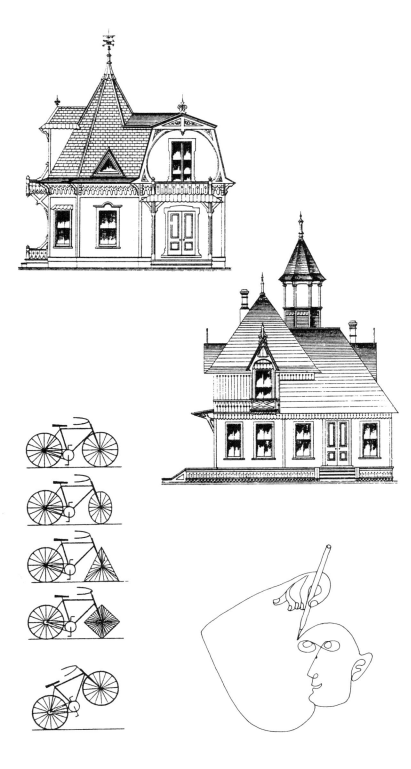

Since the Renaissance, architecture and art have been considered something outside of life. When wealthy persons wanted houses they retained architects. The clients described their wants and the architects designed a shell around a caricature of their lives. We can now see that the life is the resource. The designer can create a mechanism for family life which shapes itself to the family's living patterns.

We can no longer visualize architecture as a finished product, but instead as a catalyst, a shoehorn that helps people put on shoes, or grease on the skids that help to move a heavy weight. Architecture can now be conceived of as a mechanism that helps channel energy into its eventual form, and is thought of in other terms, such as those proposed by Richard Bender in a comparison with photography.

Bender points out that the photographs of our fathers and grandfathers were carefully posed. Concealed rods and rests held in their heads and arms in place and lights were carefully adjusted for effect. The photographer created a composition and froze it on film. If it was a good composition, then the photograph was beautiful. If it was poor, it clearly showed the strain of people held in uncomfortable positions.

Today, when a person goes to a photographer, lights are adjusted and the photographer tells the subject to walk, talk, and move. A number of pictures are taken. The photographer offers a selection of varied photographs from which the subject can choose. The mood, expression, content of the photograph is the decision of the photographed, rather than the photographer.[2]

This is the view we will take of the art of building. We do not seek ideas that say to the subject, "hold still and we will compose you into something beautiful," but rather those in which designers use their skills to aid the subjects in selecting compositions of their own choosing. The measure of the success of design is how well the designer uses the skill he or she possesses in the service of others realizing themselves. The more successful the designer, the less evidence there will be of their activity.

The individual

The dwelling

INDUSTRIALIZED METAL HOUSE ASSEMBLY
(Photo courtesy of Aluminum Co., of America)

industrializing the wrong process

Indifferent mass housing is not the inevitable result of the division of labor that has given us the assembly line and the industrial designer. Dutch architect John Habraken has proposed a gentle judo in which the overwhelming surge of industrial standardization is turned to provide choice instead of enforced conformity.[3]

Habraken specifies that three conditions must be present for a convivial relationship between people and their dwellings to exist if they are to grow together into a living healthy city. These are freedom to combine, renewal of the elements and their surroundings, and time for a community to form and flourish. All three are now prevented by the unresponsiveness of industrial products to individual initiative. The only areas of our cities that possess their own character are the city slums.

It must be possible for urban places to be born and grow old without becoming obsolete. There must be places that accommodate the latest devices, but that still have an old history in which people live for generations and simultaneously encourage change.

The thousands of incidental, whimsical, and elusive imprints left on the places where people live are evidence that a dwelling can have no preconceived design or form. Dwellings are where people live and they become dwellings by the act of people living there. A place, a town, a village, or a city is the outcome of a way of thinking. The smallest social entity is the individual, and the place that the individual lives and works is the smallest compound. If individuals are free to combine, renew, and grow old, then the city grows in every living cell.

If the uniqueness of the occupant is ignored and individuals are reduced to standardized design criteria for the purpose of systematic analysis for the convenience of the design and manufacture of mass-produced, industrialized products, then the town cannot renew itself. Aninymous places are tied to anonymous building blocks, set in place in the town plan to form part of a larger regional plan, in which change must take place in blocks and cannot occur individually.

The town or city is then always composed of areas which are new or old. A building crisis always exists which is always remedied by building products. The only way that the occupants can impress their stamp on their surroundings is to wear them down. The system itself generates a continual state of emergency.

HOUSING BUILT FOR SQUATTERS, VANDALIZED
AND ABANDONED, BRAZIL 1979
BRAZILIAN MOUNTAINSIDE SQUATTER
COMMUNITY, 1979
(Courtesy of Gilda and Vic Bonardi)

It is not industrialization, but its application, that Habraken pleads must be changed. The reintroduction of individual choice as an active element in the design of living places is the key to the application of industrialization.

A standardized, uniform way of life is not the inevitable result of the industrial process. It is the result of a way of thinking that existed long before standardization dominated industrial work. Housing built for industrial workers at the very beginning of the Industrial Revolution, before industrial production had been fully developed, was built on standardized models. And, as of yet, no attempt has been made to concentrate on individual choice as the logical result of the industrial apparatus.

Choice, Habraken believes, is compatible with the principle of industrial production. To achieve it the occupant's role and the role of the society as a whole must be defined. Individual adjustment to a place is a communal act that takes place within a framework influenced by community requirements. Adjustment cannot occur exclusively in either sphere. Barracks and prisons are total communal living. Living in an exclusively individual sphere is equivalent to exile. Today individual choice in dwellings and work places has almost disappeared. The individual is permitted a limited selection of furniture, floor coverings, and curtains in his house. A few potted plants and pictures on the wall are permitted in the office. These are very small choices within the range of those possible.

At the opposite extreme, in the barriada, squatter settlement, beach community, and campsite, everything occurs in the sphere of the individual with no aid from the community. In either instance the extreme is not determined by industrial production, but is instead the result of organization. The problem is not technical, but lies in the view of the organization of technology.

Industrial productivity can be utilized to encourage choice if introduced from the beginning. If the division between community and individual is defined and choice is extended to the realm of the individual, industrial productivity and individual action can be combined.

All building today is carried out by mechanized building trades with no distinction between the community and the individual. The same design techniques, builders, and building products are applied to apartment houses, department stores, skyscrapers, service stations, pizza parlors, and individual houses.

(Courtesy of General Motors Corp.)

Industrial
production

BUCKMINSTER FULLER DOME, EXPO MONTREAL

Mechanized
Building

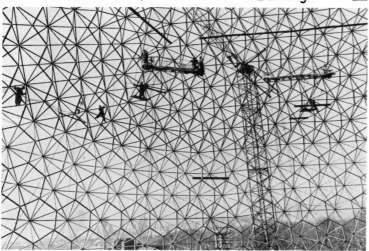

The industrial system and the architectural system that combine in building are distinctly different. In industrial production the product is mobile, the production system stationary. In the building system the product is stationary, the system mobile. Living places are the result of both systems.

The industrial system supplants the architectural system wherever the two come in contact. For example, the fireplace was originally part of the stationary architectural system. It has been replaced by stoves and furnaces, which are part of the industrial system. Cupboards, which were once built into the building as closets and pantries, have been detached from the architectural system and have become part of an industrial system of ready-made cabinets. The industrial system serves as the producer of consumer goods for the architectural system.

If the architectural and the industrial systems are extended, we will find that in the sphere of the community everything used collectively can be produced as part of the stationary architectural system. In the sphere of the individual, everything used individually can be manufactured as part of the industrial system.

The two systems are delineated by the nature of choice. Communal decisions are slow, individual decisions impulsive. Where multiplicity of choice is possible, personal identification is invariably expressed through both systems.

This view of industrialization creates a natural distinction between the public and the private sectors of building. The public authority is responsible for planning and building support structures. The private sector is responsible for developing industries geared to producing a variety of dwelling parts to fit within the supports.

The supports, the architectural framework for communal use, consists of everything used collectively--foundations, roofs, staircases, and plumbing and electrical systems. The detachable units include all that come within the occupant's range of decision and are not necessarily industrial products. In principle a brick wall can be a detachable unit if the wall's location is decided by the individual occupant. There are thus two distinct systems. They are the result of two distinct streams of production.

SUPERSTRUCTURE, THEME PAVILLION
EXPO MONTREAL, 1967
(Courtesy of Expo. Corp.)

Mass housing

WALL OF DOORS, GREECE (Courtesy of Ted Naos)

There are also two design systems. One is that of the supports, which are carefully planned and designed by architects and engineers to satisfy the dictates of the community. The other is the spontaneous design of the occupants. This is design by adaption, where the recognition of the object and its possible use occur simultaneously. If one use does not prove workable, then there are as many other uses as the individual can conceive.

Together the supports and detachable units are assembled to form a living place. The distinction gives rise to the possibility of developing new products that encourage personal choice, with emphasis on the function of the element, rather than on a preconceived form.

In both spheres, that of the support and that of the detachable unit, the product has its own use time and wear life. The support bridges and connects generations. A community takes over what is left behind from previous generations, uses, changes, and passes it on. Detachable units are bought impulsively as they appeal because of their style, improvement of product, price, and all of the egocentric whims people indulge while fitting themselves to their surroundings. The distinction between the personal and the communal spheres makes possible their combination.

The concept of a set of detachable units as a collection of consumer goods influences the form of the supports. The criteria for a good support is based on its ability to create a great number of combinations through the use of a minimum number of detachable units.

In the production of detachable units a direct relationship of choice occurs between the individual consumer and the product as it does in the production and sales of other consumer goods. All the inherent advantages, such as choice based on price, quality, taste, and requirement, are present, as well as the inherent dangers, such as influencing the consumer to purchase useless and sometimes dangerous commercial artifacts. This aspect of industrial production does not change. Individual responsibility and choice, together with their inherent dangers, have been extended.

Design is vital for an architecture of choice, but this is not the design of appearances. At best, architects design buildings termed "architecture"; they never form the people inside of them. Architecture can frustrate or encourage the human will to form; it cannot substitute for it.

BITS AND PIECES
FRENCH QUARTER, NEW ORLEANS

The designer can translate a person's longing for a home
or pleasant work place into productional feasibility. A
personal place is not a thing that can be designed by another.
It is an act of spontaneous design, of found objects, of
atavistic urges, and of instantaneous recognition of the right
juxtaposition of objects. The function of the designer is
that of providing "found objects" that can be used in the
greatest variety of ways for the individual's personal discoveries. It is at this point that the designer's creativity
ends and the individual's creativity begins.

Habraken's peculiar genius has been to interpret what he
saw. Proof of his conclusions are all around us. For example,
the "Old Quarter" of New Orleans, known as the "French Quarter,"
has no French buildings. Somehow it has retained a freedom to
combine and renew itself and has found time to grow old through
French, Spanish, and American occupations. In houses and work
places the newest appliances are continually substituted within
old frameworks. The community accommodates merchants, housewives, bars, and laundromats. It retains itself despite the
influx of hundreds and thousands of year-round tourists, more
devastating than any of its previous occupations, and even
seems to gain sustenance from it. There are similar incipient
communities in Atlanta, San Francisco, New York City, and
probably some can be found in Peoria, Illinois, and perhaps
even Columbus, Ohio.

In New York City the old concrete frame condominiums have
furnished the supports for constant individual tenant adjustment. Rooms are bought and sold by occupants on the same
floor, above and below. Living spaces are rearranged and
adjusted to increases in family size, affluence, and whim.
These strong redundant structures are living models of
Habraken's supports. The principle evolved accidentally in
New York was purposefully repeated in Hong Kong, where concrete
infrastructures are filled in by the occupants, who adjust
them as their limited resources allow.

Habraken's three principles seem part of the natural behavior
of humankind. Behind their crumbling fronts, old houses are constantly renewed. In slums and worn down rural areas the latest
appliances and industrial products are installed, as they can be
afforded, and the supports shored up as best they can be. Wherever
cracks in the monolithic facade of industrial indifference occur,
the three elements--freedom to combine, the opportunity to renew,
and time for community to form and flourish--are seized upon and
exploited.

building with the wrong materials

Not only are we industrializing the wrong process, but we are building with the wrong materials. Some of the most inventive structures built during the past two decades were made of materials that would never, by any stretch of the imagination, have been listed in building manufacturer's catalogs.

We know that the Egyptians built pyramids, the Greeks temples, the Romans aqueducts, and the medieval clerics cathedrals. Each of these building passions bankrupted the society that built them. Twentieth-century technology and design contribute to the historic bankruptcy tradition by erecting monumental garbage heaps. Bubble gum wrappers last longer than the bubble gum they protect. No-deposit bottles from one bush-league baseball game would fill the majestic nave of most thirteenth century cathedrals. Styrofoam packed monthly around cosmetic shipments to a modest midwest department store is larger in bulk than Cheopes' great pyramid at Giza and is almost as lasting a material. Our garbage heaps are the bankrupting monuments of our time. Yet there are those who would, by an inversion of technology, convert our garbage heaps to gold mines.

The garbage-heap miners of the counterculture and some "far out" architects have built structures from scavenged materials that are masterpieces of imaginative design, technology, and building form.

The ideas that spawned a garbage architecture in North America are a time-honored custom in less-developed countries. Returning veterans of "bush fire" wars invariably remark on the tidiness of the battlefields picked clean of debris before the smoke of battle clears. The ideologies that are bled and died for do not last as long as the industrial refuse generated by the battles. The legacy bequeathed so-called "backward nations" is not that of western democracy but of tin-can cups, beer-can roofs, oil-drum siding, and shell-casing cooking utensils. In the underindustrialized world the discards of western technology become ingeniously worked treasures.

The possibilities in dump material was rediscovered by the "counterculture" during the 1960s. Thousands of industrial-discard building experiments were conducted. Some were quite sophisticated and others were little more inventive than the "Hooverville" shacks erected during the Great Depression. The foundations of an indigenous architecture were layed in the 1960s, and most of the building materials used were gleaned from garbage dumps.

→ Pattern ←

→ REVERSE GARBAGE TRUCK ←

CONTEXT: A PRIMARY SCHOOL DISTRICT

SOLUTION: The truck: a vehicle that roams the region picking up scrap material for children's craft play. The truck makes regular rounds to schools, to drop off its haul, or to demonstrate its latest discovery. Sometimes kids ride around in the truck - turning it into a school on wheels - to make the pick ups.

PROBLEM: There is never enough material around schools which can truly enrich the child's learning/play environment; at the same time, throughout most urban regions, a fantastic quantity of scrap material goes to waste: paper, wood, surplus parts, gadgets, building materials, fabric, etc. Teachers are always having to go out on their own time and collect materials which will be new and interesting. The reverse garbage truck solves this problem. At the same time it provides a chance for children to go out on field expeditions - scavenger hunts - to find the material. The truck then goes from school to school letting teachers and children make selections from its latest finds.

PAGE FROM "ADVERTISEMENTS FOR A COUNTER CULTURE" PROGRESSIVE ARCHITECTURE JUNE, 1970
DETAIL OF INFLATED STRUCTURE, FREEMONT, CALIFORNIA 1970 (Photo by F. Wilson)

The counterculture accepted poverty as a mystic experience. Building with an affluent society's discards proved a practical symbolic act of protest. These builders were better trained and not as hungry as the poor of Asia, Africa, or America.

At the Freestone, California conference in March, 1970 "the reverse garbage truck," was proposed by Sim Van der Ryn's Farallone Institute. Van der Ryn, who later became the state architect for California, proposed a vehicle that would roam the region, picking up scrap material and delivering it to the schools for children's craft play. Schools, it was pointed out, invariably lack enough material to enrich the children's learning and play environment. Meanwhile, a great quantity of scrap material goes to waste in an industrial society. The reverse garbage truck program was organized as a scavenger hunt. The truck went from school to school, offering a variety of discarded materials for children and teachers to select and build from. The intention was not innocent. The reverse garbage truckers believed that children who experienced the joy of building in grammar school would be much less inclined to accept the standardized mind-numbing education meted out to them in schools.

In Domebook II, Bob Easton writes of a "scrounged dome" of considerable size built at a cost of thirty-five dollars. Ken Kern's book, Owner Built Home, mirrors the theme of spontaneous design and describes the philosophy of scavenger builders:

> *A perceptive scavenger is able to envision the use of unusual material in his prospective dwelling merely because his vision of the structure is both unorthodox and flexible. He lets the materials contribute to the design and form, rather than discarding the materials or attempting to form it into a preconceived mold. The exercise of ingenuity and the challenge that goes with the utilization of waste material can be a dominant motivation to the artistic personality....[4]*

Kern has described what was previously outlined in our discussion of design as the act of found or spontaneous design. Most of the designs of the "counterculture" followed this pattern.

Kern proposed that the serious scavengers avail themselves of the tools of sophisticated technology. Welding equipment was essential for the mining of scrap metal in the local dump. He also tells of the virtues of broken sidewalks as pavement blocks, of used telephone poles, railroad ties, packing crates, and of worn-out lithographic plates.

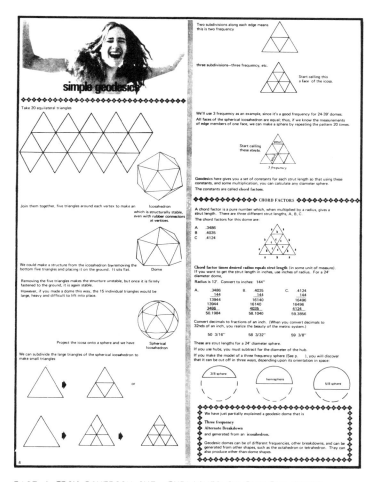

PAGE 4 FROM DOMEBOOK ONE, PUBLISHED BY PACIFIC DOMES,
LOS GATOS, CALIFORNIA

FORM FOLLOWS FUNCTION, FREESTONE, CALIFORNIA, 1970

The counterculture, which for a very short time promised to create a new American architecture, was remarkable for technical innovation and building with crusading zeal. It possessed all the attributes of an original architecture. The counterculture exercised the necessary intolerance and zeal to create new forms. It assigned spiritual meaning to these new forms and encouraged innovation and the free dispersal of building knowledge.

The movement was marked by a mixture of sophisticated and simple technology and the quick acquisition of craft and working skills. The counterculture builders were the exact opposite of the rich in tradition and the poorly schooled builders of Africa, Asia, and South and North America. They were remarkably rich in education, with no building tradition at all except what they were able to scrape together during the decade of their existence. In many instances the complex mathematics of the domes were reduced to simple coefficients. As a result, imaginative dome structures were built by teenagers and previously unskilled builders. In almost all instances, men, women, boys, and girls worked together.

It was from this ambience that Martin Pawley's "Garbage Housing" proposals emerged. Pawley, an architect and journalist, researched and formalized the concept and presented it first in the English architectural magazine, Architectural Design, and later in a small pamphletlike book entitled, Garbage Housing. Garbage was elevated to the status of learned research in the architectural curriculums of Cornell, Rensellaer, and Florida A and M Universities, where Pawley served as professor.[5]

Pawley claimed that productivity rates of the multinational consumer industries far outstripped those of building product manufacturers. In terms of the staggering need for world building, industrial products, therefore, afforded a rational supply of material for the worldwide building needs. Industrial productivity could be linked to building by developing building systems that used existing industrial products, rather than endeavoring to invent a new building industry based on our present concepts of building technologies, Pawley claimed. An altered view sees garbage as the treasure of building technology.

In a reversal of the traditional building sequence, in which the industrially rich leave their discards for the use of the ingenious poor, Pawley explored the possibilities of consciously building and designing with the products of mass-production industries.

TOMB STONE/HEAD LIGHT, GEORGIA SEACOAST
(Photo by John Sheperd)

ROADSIDE HUBCAP MERCHANDISING IN RURAL GEORGIA
(Photo by John Shepherd)

The point is not the present performance of the structures so far constructed, but in the principle itself. Products such as cans are produced worldwide on a tremendous scale. Pawley contends that metal can production in the United States alone annually runs to about eighty billion units. In a hypothetical projection using ten thousand cans to build an average house, eight million can houses could be built each year. Brick production, on the other hand, runs to about eight billion units a year, sufficient to build only one-tenth of this number.

The purpose of Pawley's research is not to propose that houses be built exclusively of either bricks or cans. But he does point out that the production of expendable steel containers, organized on automated production methods, operates at ten times the capacity achieved by bricks, which is a roughly comparable building material. In further support of his contention, Pawley points out that the cost of each can, although submerged in factors such as capitalization, volume, and demand, is estimated at half that of each brick, and if retrieved from the garbage dumps, where six million tons of steel from this source is tipped into landfill annually, it costs nothing.

In this view of industrialization an enormous variety of mass-produced items suddenly becomes "found objects." All of the consumer industries, from the container and packing industries through television sets and motor vehicles, demonstrate the possibility of becoming building materials.

These products are industrially formed like building materials from steel, aluminum, glass, plastics, wood, and synthetic compounds. They are produced, distributed, and finally disposed of on a worldwide scale infinitely larger than that which is achieved by even the simplest and most widely used building materials. They could also be employed without interfering with current industrial rates of productivity.

Pawley's view also demonstrates that, in one context at least, the development of industrial production capability might already have moved beyond dependence upon the materials of the traditional building-products manufacturers. It also points toward a process of integrative design and technique as a key to the merging of consumer industry levels of productivity with crucial building need.

HOUSE DESIGNED AND CONSTRUCTED OF INDUSTRIAL WASTE MATERIALS
BY ARCHITECT MARTIN PAWLEY AND HIS STUDENTS AT RENSSELAER
INSTITUTE, TROY, NEW YORK (Courtesy of Martin Pawley)

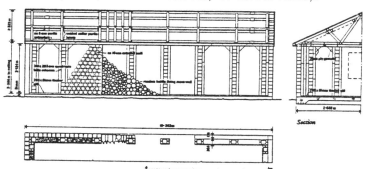

Section

Details, plan and elevation of south wall

Pawley's work and that of other "garbage designers," have found acceptance as an art form. The ultimate test, that of publication in <u>Domus</u>, the leading "haute couturier" magazine of design, has been accorded them.[5]

However the primary importance of the process, whether employed by avant-garde architects, sophisticated counter-culture builders, or Mexican camposinos, is in the altered view of established values that promote and encourage the possibility of new combinations. The field of building invention is thrown open to all comers, from those who hold Masters of Architecture degrees to ghetto delinquents. No material can escape consideration as a housing possibility, as baled hay and prarie sod were once used by the pioneers for houses; anything that can be found in our industrial society is a possible building block. This view of material meets Illich's criteria, for industrial discards are as free and as ubiquitous as adjectives in advertising copy. It introduces the principle of spontaneous found design to the products of industrial production by rendering them valuable, just as primitive man and women found use in rocks and bones.

It is a design view that challenges the established patterns that industrial imperatives so rigidly enforce. It restores intelligence to work because it challenges the fixed ideas of the design professions, in which new building and design information is invariably channeled into old frames of reference. The trained designer and the untrained share-cropper are equal as builders. The ragpicker can seek professional status as an environmental resource miner, the bottle washer as stained-glass craftsman.

But the most important factor in this inversion of technology lies in Eric Hoffer's words quoted in the beginning of this book.[6] "We have as yet no expertise of talent-mining, but must wait for chance to wash nuggets out of hidden veins." The mining of scrounged materials changes building from the no-trespassing, off-limits activity, controlled by the building products manufacturers, as the major mining corporations, and returns it to the ubiquitous sour doughs with their sluce pans.

What to look forward to in fashion this year

•Vogue's Point of View

(Courtesy of Skidmore, Owings and Merrill)

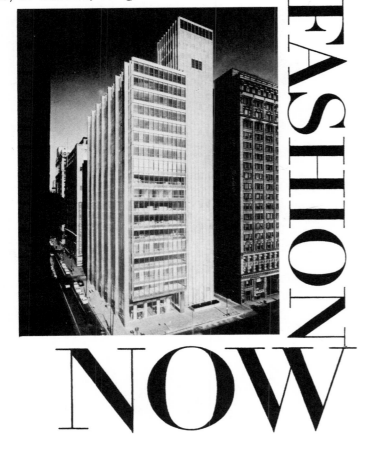

FASHION NOW

The overwhelming standardization of the automotive industry has often been proposed as the paradigm for the industrialization of our built surroundings. With this in mind, a massive competition was launched by the US Department of Housing and Urban Development in the late 1960s. It was termed "operation breakthrough." Despite the grand display of engineering and architectural virtuosity demonstrated by the hundreds of entries in the competition, very little change resulted from this much publicized major effort in the housing field. The housing industry was not revolutionized.

There are, however, other models of industrialization that fit housing needs more exactly than do those of the automotive industry, despite the claims of Le Corbusier and George Romney. One of these is that of the clothing industry. Mass-produced clothing accommodates a tremendous variation in human dimension--fat and thin, short and tall, men, women, boys, girls, young and old. The capability of the highly industrialized clothing industry offers an alternative to that of the overwhelming standardization of the automotive industry.[7]

Industrialization moved through all of its various stages in weaving. The skill of the tailor was divided into sewers and cutters; and designers came into being to coordinate their various tasks. The designer appeared in the clothing industry in much the same relationship to the clothes wearer as did the architect in the home-building industry to the occupant of the home. Both are stylists.

The annual showings of the couturiers in Paris are published worldwide. They influence the style of mass clothing manufacture in very much the same way that the architectural magazines, by publishing the work of a few architects, publicize new fashions to the architectural community. The designers set the styles, the manufacturer manufactures them, and a network of organizations create demand for the styles manufactured.

When designers first emerged they were aware of peoples' needs and preferences and created their designs to satisfy them. Clothing design was as regional as architectural styles, and both changed very slowly. As clothing industries increased in size and operations expanded, consumption of clothing had to be stimulated to increase the market. Designers changed their designs seasonally to create demand for their products to support this expanded investment.

JACQUARD LOOM THAT WEAVES PATTERNS
FROM PUNCHED CARDS WAS FIRST DISPLAYED
BY JOSEPH MARIE JACQUARD AT THE
INDUSTRIAL EXHIBITION IN PARIS IN 1801. THE
PROCESS, WHICH PREDATES THE USE OF PUNCHED
CARDS IN THE COMPUTER INDUSTRY, IS STILL USED
AND HAS COUNTLESS APPLICATIONS. RICHARD BENDER
PROPOSED THE USE OF PUNCHED CARDS IN THE
BUILDING INDUSTRY IN 1970 IN HIS BOOK
A CRACK IN THE REAR-VIEW MIRROR: A VIEW OF
INDUSTRIALIZED BUILDING. (Photographs of
loom Circa 1936 and punched cards courtesy
of American Textile Manufacturers Inst. Inc.)

Clothing manufacturers increasingly industrialized their working operation, moving from the hand cutting of materials with scissors to the use of power hand-tools that cut fifty garments at the same time. We can find similar developments in the building industry. Builders adopted the hand-held circular saw, power-driven staplers to take the place of nailing, and power-driven, hand-held planers and moulders. The computer entered both industries as it did most others as a bookkeeping tool used for payrolls and inventories.

This quickly changed as computers were introduced directly into the production process. There are now computer-driven laser beams, controlled numerically by the clothing industry, that cut single garments guided by a punched tape. No two garments need be alike and, at any future date, the machine can again read the tape and cut a garment or a piece of a garment identical to the one cut before. In some areas of building, similar computer-driven machines are used for the manufacturing of building elements, such as trusses, doors, and windows.

Industrial machines such as these are expensive. Once a company has committed itself to such an investment, has employed designers and salesmen, and has acquired a material inventory sufficient to operate on a major scale, it becomes subject to the rules of all large industries, which are established by the marketplace. The industries must grow to find the resources that will optimize their production and must continue their growth in order to guarantee the expanded market required by their expanded size. They merge with material manufacturers to assure the flow of products and merge with retail outlets to control marketing.

This pattern can be detected in the development of building products manufacturers. Large lumber companies moved into house building and eventually into tract building. They own timberlands which they clear for housing lots, then use the lumber from the lots to manufacture houses. As industries move from family businesses to corporations and conglomerates, they tend to assure their markets by leaving less to chance, choice, or coincidence. They become increasingly efficient in their own terms and move further from the ability to adjust to the idiosyncrasies of the user's need and preference. But in both clothing and housing, conflicts have developed between the user's preference and the industry's need for monolithic decision making. Designers no longer dictate fashion. There is a consumer resistance to both clothing style and housing styles.

These Days   You Are What   You Wear

ILLUSTRATION FROM THE WASHINGTON POST JANUARY, 1979

CONVERTIBLE, VERSATILE HOME SEWING MACHINE FOR VINYLS, FAKE FURS, VELOURS AND BONDED FABRICS, DESIGNED BY HENRY DRYFUS ASSOCIATES, NEW YORK CITY. (Domus Magazine)

130

In the opposition to this monolithic decision-making, which seeks to impose standardized products upon the user, a network of magazines, shops, and information centers that sell patterns, materials, tools, and instructions for self-help clothing manufacture has come into being. Home sewing machines have diminished in size and increased in complexity of performance. It is possible to buy all that is needed to make one's own clothing, from materials to design patterns. Similarly, the lumberyard and manufacturers of small machine tools have met the demand of self-help builders. The lumberyard serves the self-help builder in much the same fashion as the neighborhood sewing store helps the home sewer.

A Saturday visit to the local lumberyard or an old-fashioned hardware store will find employees giving the same kind of instruction to the home craftsman that the lady in the sewing store gives to the person about to make a garment. Lumberyards sell all the parts for home alteration. They provide shopping baskets for supplies and instruction booklets. Some even conduct free classes on various building techniques, such as floor tiling, roofing, plumbing, and electrical repair. A person wishing to alter, change, or improve his home can find everything that is needed to do so, from building materials to building information.

As the building and clothing industries became larger and monolithic and sought to stimulate sales and assure the consumption of standardized products, a parallel organization of choice also emerged. Choice is now possible on two levels, through self-help and through the development of mass-produced individual items using the capabilities of computers and laser beams. Sophisticated technology can be devoted to individual choice, as well as the infliction of standardization. It is no accident that bookstores sell fifty times as many books on how to do things--from building your own yurt to macrame--than they do on architectural design.

Clothing as shelter

RECEPTION AREA, CONNECTICUT GENERAL. FURNITURE BY KNOLL INTERNATIONAL NEW YORK CITY. (Photo by Ezra Stoller courtesy of Knoll International)

DERRING MILLIKEN OFFICES, NEW YORK CITY. FURNITURE BY KNOLL INTERNATIONAL NEW YORK CITY. (Photo by Scott Hyde courtesy of Knoll International)

the myth of mess

A change in the ideas of design can be found in the most autocratic of work places--that of the business office. The activity which we now call "interior design" did not exist as a separate design discipline before the Second World War. During the period of the Great Depression of the 1930s, offices were crowded. They were usually painted brown up to four feet above the floor and then painted an institutional green above that to conceal the dirt. Lighting was dim, amenities minimal, and people competed with each other for the privilege of working long hours amid these bleak surroundings.

After World War II conditions changed radically. Affluence, the shortage of office help, and an increased demand for office workers as automation reversed the ratio of white to blue collar workers combined to force the birth of what we now term "interior design."

Office workers came under the scrutiny of industrial psychologists, efficiency experts, and industrial designers, as industrial workers had suffered similar attentions half a century earlier. Corporations were forced to compete for the supply of knowledge workers and tried to increase their efficiency and the attractiveness of their surroundings.

As a result, work places became hygienic, clean, dry, well lit, safe, temperature controlled, and absolutely sterile. Clutter was eliminated and workers were assigned fixed work positions in relation to their productive importance, as management conceived this importance to be. Major executives were assigned corner offices and minor executives offices with numbers of windows corresponding to their rank in the corporate hierarchy. Partition height, desk size, floor and window coverings became status symbols rigidly prescribed by management and diligently adhered to by interior designers. Secretaries were arranged in orderly assembly-line rows. Designers layed out offices as engineers had previously designed industrial work places. But office workers did not become more productive. The malaise of office workers, like sabotage on the assembly line, became and remains a management frustration.

The working office is rarely considered to be a place of beauty. Serious effort is made to clear away the evidence of work before offices are photographed as design accomplishments. In contrast to this, cowboys, electricians, chefs, football players, telephone linemen, construction workers--all those who exercise freedom of movement in the performance of their tasks--manage to present evidences of their work attractively.

131

IBM 8775 DISPLAY TERMINAL AND
OPERATOR (Courtesy of IBM)

ENTRANCE TO ARCHITECTS OFFICE, TORONTO, CANADA

Designers seldom live or work in the places they design. The designer who proclaimed the virtue of the precise alignment of office elements, the elimination of superfluous decoration, white immaculate surfaces, bright uniform lighting, in the precise logic of Mondrian, usually lived in a period house and worked in a nondescript office surrounded by clutter.

The workers who process information in offices tend to work just as the designer does in his or her private life. They adjust their work spaces and artifacts to suit their own unique creative processes, and, if allowed, live and work in creative clutter.

It is only the top executives, who do not work in their offices, who take pride in exhibiting their offices as feats of design. Executives work in boardrooms, meeting rooms, expensive restaurants, on airplanes, golf courses, and in personal contact with their subordinates, who work in set work positions.

The working environment of office workers is of vital importance to information production, yet the condition of their surroundings is a paradox. The more interesting the work, the more oblivious the worker is of his or her surroundings. Clutter is part of our folklore. The absent-minded professor, the artist, and the writer who forget to don their trousers are jokes about people who are so preoccupied with their work that they forget their physical and personal surroundings. A good worker is driven by purpose and takes little notice of surroundings. Only overt obstructions are taken into consideration.

There are a number of fanciful conclusions concerning what constitutes the ideal environment for knowledge work. It was only through considerable research experiment and experience that Robert Probst, designer for Herman Miller, was able to reach what he considered rational conclusions concerning office work.[8] He claims our concept of work places has proven counterproductive. The compelling tensions that everyone faces in organizational living is in a continuing struggle for identity. Knowledge workers must constantly reassure themselves of who they are and what they are doing. Successful surroundings are those that allow this need to be expressed by conveying identity information.

The tendency to "mess up the place" is the occupant's imprint. Working mess is a visual identity of tasks and areas of responsibility. Work artifacts are the feedback notations that remind the occupant of the spaces of their involvements in their tasks. They are keys to what the occupant knows, rearrangeable signals in the structure of the occupant's thinking process.

MESS AS ART, LOBBY SCULPTURE IN SEARS TOWER, CHICAGO, ILLINOIS
(Courtesy of Skidmore, Owings and Merrill Architects)

OFFICE FOR IBM 705 COMPUTER
(Courtesy of IBM Corporation)

Work clutter appears despite the designer's deliberate effort to suppress it. If the space cannot be personalized and possessed by its occupant, it will be abandoned or the occupant will lose interest in the tasks at hand. Places that stimulate the worker are developed, elaborated, and preserved by appropriate use. Evidence of possession can be concealed or eliminated, but the penalty in efficiency is enormous.

Probst found that knowledge work operates the most efficiently when based on worker-generated arrays of papers and objects. Though they may appear disorderly to the passing observer and absolutely repugnant to the designer, they are in fact collections of subtle feedback signals that sustain the process of the work. The clutter of work is in reality a visual information system of flags, signals, and cueing devices. These direct physical notations help the knowledge worker adjust to an increasing overabundant information supply. It gives a more realistic evaluation of his and her capacity for involvement and the relevance and importance of the information.

By making individual work areas direct information centers, less delusion is harbored about the retrieval of stored information. A very small percentage of information that leaves the work area is ever reintroduced into the work process.

The knowledge workers must establish an identity with their surroundings and display their work to reaffirm who they are and what they do in much the same fashion as those housed must establish a personal place using familiar memory objects around them.

The price paid for ignoring or suppressing either human tendency in the office or in the housing product is atrocious. When office workers cannot establish a sense of place in the world they do not destroy or vandalize their surroundings as do the occupants of housing projects, for the conditions of work are rigidly controlled. Overt destruction in the office is rare, but unproductive lethargic behavior is commonplace.

Malaise, lethargy, sabotage can be designed, but involvement, interest, motivation is self-generated. This is as true of the work place as it is of the home. The best the designer can accomplish is a working armature, upon which the housed or the worker can establish their living and working identities.

GATEWAY TO THE CITY
Liberty Street Ferry entrance to
New York City underneath the
West Side Highway (circa 1964)

SITTING AT 747 THIRD AVENUE, A WILLIAM KAUFMAN BUILDING
(Photo by Dirck Halstead courtesy Kaufman Organization)

joy in the streets

Few self-respecting children ever play in a playground. The asphalted, fenced-in playground is only an acknowledgment of the fact that the concept of play exists. It has nothing to do with play itself.

The play that children practice is located in a different place every day. It may be indoors, in a friendly gas station, by the river, in a derelict building, or on an abandoned construction site. Each play activity and the objects it requires form a system that is part of other city systems.

Play takes place in a thousand places, filling the interstices of adult life. As they play, children are prompted by cues from their surroundings. There are no clues in a fenced-in asphalted playground.

Children's play and the activities of the owner-builder are very much alike. No self-respecting owner-builder would confine himeself to the fenced-in restrictions imposed upon the architect whose professional code of ethics shuts out land speculation, financial juggling, huckstering, construction manipulation, and all the surrounding cues afforded by the social, economic, and political composition of a city. As a result, the owner-builder's activities fill the gaps in the built environment left by professional designers. He is like the child who explores every nook and cranny of the city, no matter how forbidden or how dangerous it may appear. The owner-builder is also like the Mississippi riverboat gambler in that "wherever he finds a deck of cards he lays his money down."

Yet no matter what the owner-builder's accomplishments, how audacious and successful his schemes, how inventive, creative, and beneficial to the community, he remains invisible. It was not Zechendorf, the flamboyant genius who financed and schemed to realize his visions culminating in such building projects as Place Ville Marie in Montreal and Kips Bay Plaza in New York City, who is remembered for these undertakings, but one of his employees, an architect named I. M. Pei.

The shift of vision from the architect's view of the world to that of the owner-builder's gives us a fragmented picture in which idiocy, avarice, creativity, inspiration, generosity, compassion, and egocentricity collide, fragment, and recombine in kaleidoscopic combinations.

PORT AUTHORITY BUS TERMINAL
NEW YORK CITY

SEAGRAMS BUILDING, NEW YORK CITY

It has always been claimed that the distinction between architecture and building is that architecture has a unique spirit that building does not. Architecture like all art should please, contended Herbert Read:

Any general theory of art must begin with this supposition; that man responds to the shape and surface and mass of things present to his senses, and that certain arrangements in the proportion of the shape and surface and mass of things result in a pleasurable sensation, whilst the lack of such arrangement leads to indifference or even to positive discomfort and revulsion.[9]

For most city dwellers the spirit of the city is one of "discomfort and revulsion." Despite the best of design intentions, modern cities do not have the places of magic or terror, joy or delight, which characterized human settlements of the past. They function frantically from nine to five, five days a week, and are then abandoned. The safest place to ride a bicycle in New York City, the economic capital of our nation, is in the financial district on a Sunday afternoon. Cities usually do not even provide the weary pedestrian a place to sit down. Lovers are forced to use doorways for intimate contact and casual acts of personal violence occur anywhere.

The art of the architect gives no pleasurable sensations. It provides a simple profusion of metal extrusions and cast concrete panels that form endless moire patterns, from sidewalks to cooling towers in the sky.

Buildings are either well or poorly designed, but are invariably indifferently manufactured industrial products. Their design and manufacture is the result of what Habraken described earlier as the "non-relationship" in which designer, builder and occupant are unknown to each other.

Yet there does exist a unique class of builders who are exceptions to this relationship. They are, paradoxically, the pursuers of the "fast buck" the wheelers and dealers, the real estate specialists and speculators who own the buildings they build and gamble with their money and their designs using the city as their gaming board.

ANONYMOUS BUILDING BY OWNER BUILDER, HELSINKI, FINLAND

Although these owner-builders dominate the city building scene, both they and their buildings remain almost invisible. Their works are not featured in the architectural magazines or in the art sections of the Sunday newspapers. If their buildings appear in print at all they are to be found among the ads of the real estate sections. The owner-builder's influence on the built environment is rarely acknowledged in schools of architecture, in architectural magazines, or in the reviews of the architectural critics. When noticed at all it is usually condemned by those sensitive to good taste and labeled common and vulgar, which they usually are.

It is said that architects are the professionals responsible for the quality of the buildings around us. Yet major corporations and their architects build less than ten percent of today's city buildings. Owner-builders are the major, if not the master builders of urban places.

The owner-builder commissions and controls building specialists--architects, engineers, contractors, and sub-contractors--in short the entire coterie of those responsible for the building process. He is a building juggler. He pays as little as he can for land and builds upon it as cheaply as possible. If the land is near apartment houses or offices, he builds apartments and office buildings, or factories or shopping centers. He rents or sells his property depending upon the economic advantage of doing either. If he succeeds, he becomes an "entrepreneur" or an "investor-builder." If he is rich, he is crafty; if he goes broke, he is called a fool.

Primarily, the owner-builder builds small, nondescript buildings; little garages, small factories, sixty family apartment houses, or a local shopping center without enough parking. He builds with concrete block in the back and brick in the front and exposed steel joists between. He swings with the market, and wherever he smells a dollar, that is where he goes.

There are few sins which the owner-builder has not committed. He is said to be a rotten client to the architect, a slow payer to the contractor, and a rotten landlord to his tenant. Despite all of this, owner-builders have built most of America. They did it because no one else was fast, smart, foolish enough, or had enough guts to try. Yet, no matter how imperfectly, the owner-builder is a sensitive responder to the day-by-day demands of the community and the building needs of the nation.

PAN AMERICAN BUILDING AT THE END OF A CORRIDOR OF ANONYMOUS
OWNER BUILT SKYSCRAPERS, NEW YORK CITY

To survive the owner-builder must assess accurately the physical needs of those who will use his buildings. This all too imperfect builder is often the only one responding to client need, and, in many instances, if he does not build homes, they are not built. Whatever his faults, the owner-builder reacts to client need from personal experience.

One of the most articulate owner-builders in recent years is a man named Melvyn Kaufman, a member of the William Kaufman organization. The "Organization" is a synonym for what Fortune magazine once termed one of New York City's major building "families." Kaufman's and the owner-builder's arguments forcibly demonstrate a challenge to the architectural profession on its most sacred soil, its design "turf." Kaufman states that architects do not have the ability to create city places of joy, stimulation, and terror. But beyond this he accuses them of an aggressively malicious philosophy that relegates the cities' occupants to the peripheral edges of their design creations.

What makes Kaufman's arguments so difficult for designers to counter is that he has demonstrated in words and buildings, in ideas and action, that stimulating places can be designed by his own efforts. Ironically, he has provided them in the unabashed guise of a "vulgar speculator" in pursuit of a fast buck. He demands a "double take," a second look, for his street events are always crowded. In contrast, the deserted plazas of yesterday's buildings lauded as design triumphs appear today as nothing more than pink-pilled environmental placebos.

Any owner-builder, according to Kaufman, can "design" a major office building in about two hours. The reason is simply because the building designs itself. The owner-builder wastes no time on aesthetic decisions. He has had enough experience to know the form the building must take to make the most profitable use of the city's zoning regulations. By rule of thumb calculation, land of eighteen thousand square feet or less is simply unprofitable for any New York City building.

If the land is forty thousand square feet or more, a straight tower is built. If under that, a base and a tower. The city's rules state that forty percent of the ground area can compose the square foot area of the tower floors, and floors housing mechanical equipment are not counted in the floor area ratio. The city rules will allow a bonus of ten to one square foot area if the owner-builder builds a plaza and a bonus of three to one for an arcade.

SITTERS AT KAUFMAN BUILDING, 77 WATER STREET, NEW YORK CITY (Courtesy of The Kaufman Organization)

SITTERS BENEATH DIGITAL CLOCK AT KAUFMAN BUILDING, 127 JOHN ST., NEW YORK CITY (Photo by Dirck Halstead, courtesy of Kaufman Organization)

There are fixed elements in the plan--window modules and column modules, number of stairs in relation to the floors, and the number of toilets required for the number of tenants.

In the ultimate sense the city is the architect. It builds itself through a system of rules and regulations. Cities grow because of the activity of the people in them. The rules of the city evolve; the codes, zoning regulations, and restrictions and the laws determine the form, the size, the shape, its structure, and the building style. If this is true, as every owner-builder proves daily, then what is the function of the architect, Kaufman asks?

Planners and architects have no concept of the vitality of a city, Kaufman contends. This is due either to their training or an inherent inability to understand the concept of people's freedom to grow and develop as they see fit, not by plan or control. This is the heart of Kaufman's complaint concerning the design of cities. Architects seem to be trained under a discipline which has as its basis the banishment of people to the edge of their creations, or worse, the restructuring of people to make them worthy of entering the architectural temple.

At this stage in our building history, we have developed structures of such scale that they are incomprehensible to the pedestrian. The closer their proximity to the person in the street, the more remote they appear. The ghastly scale tends to render the individual insignificant. It is, therefore, the responsibility of the builder to make as little of the building as possible, since the building is so overbearing, inhuman, and irresponsible to the burden it places on the passing individual. The responsibility of the designer, the builder, and the owner is to make the building disappear. This is Kaufman's design imperative. The objective should be to develop more static canyon walls in the hope that they will look as much as possible like the walls around them. In this way instead of overwhelming the onlooker he or she can ignore them.

There is no virtue in trying to uplift the spirits of the people in the street by great thoughts or schemes. Kaufman's desire is only to befriend and make people comfortable. The goal is to give the person in the street joy, excitement, and pleasure of their own making within the parameters of their own values. "People must be drawn out of the shell they develop as a defense against passing through the behavioral sink forced upon them each day in their route from home to office," he says.

SITTERS AT KAUFMAN BUILDING, 77 WATER STREET, NEW YORK CITY
(Photo by Dirck Halstead, courtesy of Kaufman Organization)

LONELY SITTER, NEW YORK CITY

The Owner-Builder Entrepreneur

Long ago, Kaufman discarded the idea of instructing people as to what is "good," "art," or what is "tasteful." "People do very well without my instruction," he concluded. "I absolutely refuse to impose my opinion of what is good taste or bad, except as an alternative. I refuse to instruct people that the building they are entering is important. It is they that are important."

"Architects fail," Kaufman contends," when they ask the client to adjust. Today's client is the city's common people with common taste. It is the architect and not the client who must adapt himself.

There is no point in building any kind of place if it is not built for people. If the architect is commissioned to design a monkey house he would talk to the zookeeper and would be told his needs. The architect would build a place called a "monkey house." But the purpose would be for people to live and work with monkeys. "The monkeys don't want the house."

Kaufman's theme has the familiar ring of that popularized by segments of the architectural profession during the 1960s under the stirring manifesto "architecture for people." This popular slogan was filtered through the architectural schools and magazines and emerged institutionalized into the systematic design parameters we now term "user need" studies.

The difference is that in reality and retrospect our view of idealism and avarice is inverted. The large-scale idealistic professional enthusiasm of the "peoples' architects" provided no small-scale popular amenities. Now the peoples' architects seem content to rest on their laurels while most of the city's people continue to sit on fire hydrants.

Kaufman, the owner-builder, in his pursuit of "a fast buck" did provide places of wonder and excitement, small festivals in the streets. What Kaufman has done is not architecture as architecture is defined, but it has proven more valuable, at least until the Vitruvian concepts of firmness, commodity, and delight provide the city's people a place to sit down.[10]

handicapping squatters

Sportsmanship is a gentlemanly attribute and we therefore expect fair play from the well born and bred. Architects and designers are gentle folk, made so by generations of association with kings, princes, prelates, and industrialists. It seems rational, therefore, that in the interest of sportsmanship, designers allow points for disadvantages when comparing their accomplishments with the efforts of those less privileged and less educated than themselves. This practice is universally accepted by rich and poor alike, from wagers placed at Suffolk Downs to hasty bets whispered in the ear of street corner bookies, and is known as handicapping.

Yet fair play is seldom found when housing is evaluated throughout the world. There is an almost universal tendency to judge the designs of architects by one standard and the buildings of the poor by another. It is true that the building efforts of those that build for themselves with very little money often appear to be random collections of discarded materials haphazardly arranged, socially costly messes that will eventually have to be replaced by tasteful planning and design. But such hasty judgment is unfair for it omits to handicap the solutions.

The building efforts of the poor, when evaluated objectively will prove to be ugly only in that poverty itself is ugly. Fairer evaluation conducted by such men as Charles Abrams and John C. Turner has demonstrated that far from causing a drain on the nation's economy that hosts them, squatters create an impressive increase in the production of housing stock and a highly successful solution to the problem of mass shelter at the very bottom economic level.

The random activity of squatting has not been confined to any one nation or even to the less industrially developed countries. It has occurred with equal impartiality on the periphery and occassionally in the center of almost every city of every continent. It took place in Britain after both the First and Second World Wars, but was confined at that time to abandoned army camps. However, the latest wave in 1968 occupied abandoned center city buildings.

During the Great Depression of the 1930s, the western United States was dotted with squatting communities composed primarily of migrant farm workers from Oklahoma, Arkansas, and Texas who were forced from their homes by dust and bank foreclosures.

RACING AT JEROME PARK, BROOKLYN, NEW YORK, 1886
(From Harper's Weekly)

SQUATTING ON THE BANKS OF THE ST. LAWRENCE RIVER,
QUEBEC, CANADA. (Photo by John Shepherd)

It was estimated that in the early 1970s there were as many as fifty thousand squatters in Britain with thirty thousand occupying buildings in London alone.[11] This was not an invasion of land common to predominantly agricultural nations, but instead the occupation of empty buildings by people without the owner's permission in the nation that gave birth to the Industrial Revolution.

The extent and nature of squatting varies in different nations and locations due to different housing situations and legal frameworks. Britain was unique in that squatting did not constitute a criminal offense. The owner of the property was forced to undertake civil proceedings against trespassers and this, in London, at the beginning of the squatter movement, required several months and was quite costly in legal fees. The time lapse was sufficient for the usurpers to establish homes and communities before the arrival of the bailiffs. Many of the properties the squatters appropriated had been purposefully wrecked and dismantled by their owners to discourage their takeover. Paradoxically, owners became the vandals and the squatters the restorers of property values. They repaired damages and in the act of doing so acquired considerable building skill.

The act of breaking the fundamental tenet of society in which private property, used or unused, is held sacred and the self-confidence of self-help changed social attitudes. A sporting evaluation of housing evidence shows that English squatters revitalized neighborhoods and repaired damaged property. The act of housing themselves which the English housing councils had failed to do might have been judged a "good show." However, the "sticky wickett" of private ownership intervened and the world-famous English reputation for fair play was drowned in a concerted press campaign of recrimination against the squatters. However, this reaction is not unusual in squatting history. The international squatter movement is accompanied by equally consistent press campaigns of condemnation. The same charges are leveled against squatters in Chili, Britain, Brazil, Manila, and Washington DC.

In reality squatters are anything but a homogeneous group of either agrarian criminals or urban gorillas. Squatter settlements include everyone from the very poor to university-trained professionals, even policemen and civil servants of the various governments that seek to evict them.

There is a marked discrepancy between the studies conducted in Peru two decades ago by John Turner, architect, and William Mangin, Professor of Anthropology at Syracuse University, and the opinions held and publicized by urban planners, architects, politicians, and newspapermen even today.

SQUATTERS NEAR CENTRAL PARK, NEW YORK CITY, 1869 (Squatters occupied this site until near the end of the century when they were driven from it by the city's northern development.) (Harper's Weekly)

MOUNTAINSIDE SQUATTER HOUSES OVERLOOKING
RIO DE JANEIRO (Courtesy of Gilda and Vic Bonardi)

The opinions most commonly voiced are that squatter settlements suffer from a predominance of social problems and are
chaotic and unorganized. It is also charged that they grow
progressively worse as time goes on and that their occupants
constitute an economic drain on the economy, flooding the cities
with unemployed families which would be better employed in rural
and agricultural pursuits. They are further labeled as criminal
havens of uncontrolled juvenile deliquency, prostitution, and
family disorganization; alienated festering pockets of life
surrounding the large urban centers.

Investigation of squatter settlements and squatter housing
from London to Peru indicates that these views are grossly inaccu-
rate. The invasion of public land was found by Turner and Mangin
to be highly organized and often conducted successfully in the
face of violent police opposition. Squatter settlements around the
world invariably form strong internal political organizations in
which thousands of people live together in orderly manner without
official community services.[12]

The original makeshift shacks constructed during the invasion
are rapidly converted into sturdy brick and cement structures. The
eventual investment in labor and material often totals millions of
dollars. It was further found by Turner and Mangin that employment
rates, wages, literacy, and educational levels were higher in the
Peruvian squatter settlement than in the central city slums from
which the squatter residents had escaped. Surprisingly enough, they
also found wage rates to be higher than the national average. Inci-
dences of crime and juvenile delinquency, prostitution, and gambling
were rare except for petty thievery, the instances of which seemed
to be smaller than in other parts of the city. The squatter settlements were remarkably opposite in almost every respect from the press
and professional views held of them.

The Peruvian squatter residents worked in the city; were
customers for city products; belonged to regional associations, sports
clubs, and civic organizations; attended movies and soccer games; and
engaged in almost all of the city's activities. They petitioned at
government offices and their children attended city schools. Their
occupations covered the entire spectrum of working activities--bank
clerk, store owner, policemen, soldier, market workers, garbage man,
seamstress, factory worker, bus driver, gardener, construction worker,
and dozens of other categories. Far from being the victims of chronic
unemployment, many families had three, four, or five members, variously
engaged in earning small incomes that in many instances amounted to
substantial sums.

142

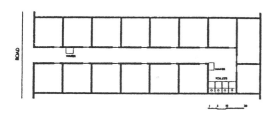

LIMA CENTRAL AREA SLUM
AFTER TURNER AND MANGIN 1957-1968

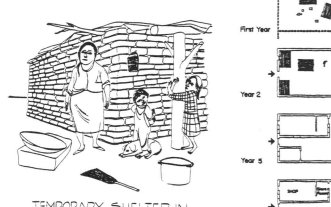

TEMPORARY SHELTER IN
BARRIADA NEAR LIMA, PERU

First Year

Year 2

Year 5

Year 15+

House Plot

SHOP | Store Room
LIVING ROOM | DINING ROOM | K | Bath | Bedrooms | Bed.

STAGES IN BARRIADA SETTLEMENT LIMA, PERU
AFTER TURNER AND MANGIN 1957-1968

BARRIADA CUERNEVACA, MEXICO (Photo by F. Wilson)

In an unbiased comparison of squatter settlements and government housing, Turner points out that the former met the requirements of the majority of the people during their periods of greatest need, and, in contrast, that government housing projects did not. They demanded high initial investments and steady payments, which placed an oppressive economic pressure on families during their development cycles. Government housing projects also prohibited any form of family adjustment to its condition through the families' own efforts, from enlarging and improving their living spaces to the establishment of small businesses or industries to improve their economic position.

The pattern of squatter settlements worldwide indicates that the first need of the unskilled and irregularly employed family with low and uncertain incomes is for a location within immediate reach of the maximum concentration and variety of job opportunities and the cheapest markets. Squatter settlements are invariably located in such a way as to satisfy both of these needs. Government housing projects, which are invariably constructed on cheap land far from the cities' vital activities, cannot satisfy these demands.

The poor realize what planners do not--that house and job are irrevocably linked. They also know by bitter experience that their wages are sporadic, depending on the vagaries of employment in peripheral jobs, while, in contrast, rents are irrevocably due at the end of stated periods.

In a study made in Delhi, India, Geoffrey K. Payne, architect and planner, found that squatter settlements invariably mushroomed on pockets of land in the inner urban areas adjacent to employment sources. They were found along the edges of railway lines and canals and were sometimes hidden behind new developments. As the settlements expanded, they filled all available space at well over one thousand people per acre.[13]

As Turner and Mangin reported from their Peruvian studies, the Indian settlements also developed strong community councils to make their peace with local politicians and to thus ensure their security of land tenure. Payne estimated that approximately twenty-five percent of the total population of Calcutta, Bombay, Delhi, and Madras were living in various types of illegal settlements.

The sporting view of squatter settlements, using the same criteria to judge them in comparison to the designs of official planners and architects, would score them remarkably high in responding to their own priorities and minimum standards.

SQUATTER HOUSES, DELHI, INDIA
(Courtesy of Dhairu Thadani)

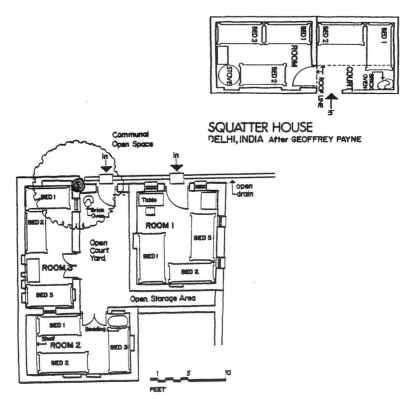

SQUATTER HOUSE
DELHI, INDIA After GEOFFREY PAYNE

SUBSTANTIAL SQUATTER HOUSE

The informal solutions of the squatters, in contrast to the deficiencies of official planning and housing programs, clearly illustrates the extent to which the measures of planners and designers have been unsuccessful in regulating the process of change. It also dramatically underscores their failure to provide acceptable shelter for the pressing needs of the poor. If we heed Charles Abrams' wise words, that worse than slums is no slums at all, then we must admit that squatter ingenuity outranks that of planners, for they have provided houses where the planners have provided none.

There is also an intrinsically basic difference in the housing provided over time. Low-cost government housing invariably deteriorates with occupancy over time, while squatter settlements beginning as miscellaneous collections of shacks and makeshift dwellings progress to substantial well-kept housing, and, if connected to city services, become prosperous city suburbs.

It is not only in the area of providing makeshift, semi-permanent or permanent shelter that squatter settlements are important, but the accomplishment itself offers a lesson to architects and planners. The site studied by Payne was developed over a period of almost forty years. It had begun as temporary structures built against a three-meter-high brick wall that separated it from railway property. As it became obvious that the existing squatters would not be moved, more families arrived and took possession. Building accelerated and spread from the original alignments in informal rows, until the full width of the site was developed.

At the time of Payne's study, the site accommodated two thousand one hundred fifty people on two acres. The density was achieved using only single-family structures and included space for grazing water buffaloes, developing cottage industries, and a variety of small, communal spaces directly related to the groups housed.

The social and spatial structures of such a settlement and its use of limited resources could yield significant insights, not only into how self-generated communities of this type evolve, but how official planning could benefit from such solutions. For a major accomplishment has taken place. A stable social order was achieved, at high densities, in an environment deficient in basic community services.

Payne's findings coincided with those of Turner in that proximity to place of work was the major determinant of locational behavior, but it did not explain fully how or why particular sites are developed.

SQUATTER SETTLEMENT, ZAMBIA
from aerial photograph

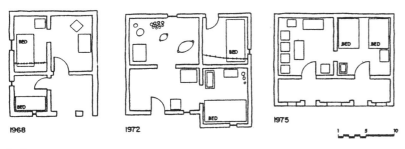

1968   1972   1975

1   5   10

RATE OF CHANGE-SQUATTER SETTLEMENT, ZAMBIA
A house on the same piece of land surveyed in 1968, 1972, 1975
AFTER RICHARD MARTIN

SQUATTER HOUSES, LAGOS, NIGERIA
(Courtesy of Rowland Ogun'Buraimoh)

However, in almost all cases, development takes place on land of limited public utility. It is either poorly drained, difficult to access, awkward in plot shapes, or located amid unattractive surroundings. Such marginally functional spaces can be found everywhere and were even available in such a rigid spacial framework as the colonial plan for New Delhi. They are ideal for squatting, since there is less chance that the construction will be noticed and ownership rights asserted.

The settlement studied by Payne represented a calculated, efficient, and imaginative use of resources in a socially acceptable form. It was a spontaneoue survival design solution using the leftovers and cast-offs of land and building material.

In a similar study in Zambia made by two architects, Paul Andrews and Richard Martin, and an economist, Malcolm Christie, it was found that only by breaking the rigid colonial rules carried over after independence was it possible for people at the lowest economic level to house themselves.[14]

Under the colonial system all decision making was restricted to whites. To maintain control of the blacks and to prevent them from doing anything that would threaten white rule a complex legal system of controls was introduced. Licenses for trading were required which restricted even such casual transactions as street vending. Free movement of persons was restricted and rigid control exerted over urban dwellings.

After Zambia gained independence in 1964, some legislation was relaxed, such as restriction on personal movement, but most of the restrictive British regulations remained in force. People were not permitted to trade from or derive money from any activity undertaken in a house. Lodgers were not permitted. Maize and bananas could not be grown on the householder's property for this was said to endanger public health.

Despite prohibitions, a network of squatter settlements emerged. Under colonial rule the vast majority of Africans were treated as migrant labor. They were forced to leave their homes and families to work in distant places. The men were allowed a few days off at the beginning of their work contract to build themselves a grass hut in the contractor's migrant labor camps. By the end of the contract period huts were often quite substantial. Contractors were expected to demolish the huts, but usually did not. People infiltrated, the compounds become permanent, and the situation was out of control.

145

SQUATTER HOUSING IN CUERNEVACA, MEXICO—BEGINNING IN THE
CAVES IN THE BACKGROUND, SHOWN IN THE UPPER PHOTO, THE
INHABITANTS MOVED TO MAKESHIFT CORREGATED IRON SHELTERS,
THESE EVENTUALLY, OVER A PERIOD OF YEARS, METAMORPHASIZED
INTO THE STURDY TWO AND THREE STORY BRICK STRUCTURES IN
THE BOTTOM PHOTOGRAPH.

There were other instances which squatters used to their
advantage, such as the practice of landowners making a profit
on otherwise unproductive land by renting out small plots for
building sites. These areas, like the contractor's camps,
also mushroomed after independence.

The situation moved beyond government control. Yet the
report by Andrews, Martin, and Christie indicates that the
settlements regulated themselves quite well. Such necessities
as water were supplied by dug wells. Those who dug shared the
water. Small industries of all kinds flourished. Building
was undertaken communally through a system of beer and work
parties. A man who had a particularly difficult and urgent
task to perform called upon his fellow villagers to assist
him. In return they were freely entertained to plentiful
beer, which his wife brewed while they worked. A highly
efficient work for thirst force could be summoned at any time.

Houses were arranged on a "decible" module spaced within
shouting distance of each other, for this is the way women
converse while doing their chores. Paths, roads, and communal
spaces were provided by the custom of mutual passage and
spontaneous gathering.

The home owners, freed from petty legislation took in
lodgers, suited the standard and size of their houses to their
pocketbooks, establish industries, and traded both large and
small. The settlements constitute, in the view of Andrews,
Martin, and Christie, a unilateral declaration of independence
from bureaucracy, its controls, and its planners.

From these three examples it would seem that a fundamental
change in professional attitudes is necessary if the spontaneous
creativity of squatter settlements is to be brought into the
communal sphere. The change involves the principle of simple
justice in which the squatters are given a sporting chance.

John Turner states that there is something desperately
wrong with the rules of the game and thinks they can be
formulated around a very simple question. Is housing to be
a function of the productivity of large organizations or a
matter of resourcefulness?

Since planners, designers, legislators, administrators,
and government officials consider housing to be a function
of industrial productivity, all building organizations
concentrate exclusively upon improving the efficiency and
productivity of increasingly large-scale industries.

SQUATTER HOUSES OAXACA, MEXICO

HOUSING PROJECT DESIGNED FOR SQUATTERS BY
STUDENTS OF THE UNIVERSITY OF MEXICO, OAXACA

Yet these industries repeatedly demonstrate their inability
to solve housing problems for the poorer classes. Their products
are too expensive, too rigidly imposed, too restrictive, and
often frustrate the very purpose they set themselves to
accomplish.

If, on the other hand, economy is the objective of the game,
with emphasis placed on the difference between capital and
income and the goal that of spending less than earned, then
large production organizations clearly score very poorly. In
fact, the more large organizations manage to produce, Turner
asserts, the less there will be to distribute to the resourceful
producers of housing.

The rules of the game of these two building methods are
entirely different. In the centralized production patterns
of large organizations decisions flow from the peak of management authority to its base. The resources that the system
controls are funneled through the system to supply goods and
services as defined categories of institutionally designed
products to institutionally defined categories of consumers.

For example, the products that are made for homeowners to
buy are designed for functions the manufacturer deems will be
useful to them and the manufacturer expends his resources to
satisfy a market his sales staff has identified. Products
are, therefore, uniform, consistent, and often quite useless.

The rules of the game of resourcefulness are exactly
opposite. Decisions are made from use, whim, inspiration,
experience, but always in intimate contact with the house and
building in much the same way that Christopher Alexander
earlier described the unselfconscious method of design.
Decisions are free to combine at will as long as decision
makers stay within the limits set by the rules established,
and we have seen that these rules are invariably established
by the squatters themselves.

The evidence is overwhelming that when people are free
of the pressures to conform, which is a freedom that given
the opportunity people will assert overnight, the variety of
choice is enormous. Choice is exerted wherever the person is
relatively free of the social pressures to conform to a rigid
norm and has the means to exert his will.

The proof of this is demonstrated in the ascending level
of control from the government housing project, descending to
the levels of increasing freedom of the squatter settlement.

POLO IN CENTRAL PARK, NEW YORK CITY 1880
(Harper's Weekly)

Turner found that the majority of people with median incomes, especially when young, were prepared to consider living in a slum in order to save for marriage, children, or a car. They might also decide to spend a higher proportion of their income on a house. The same family may jump from one priority to another at any time.

If a game is to be fair, then the variety of the rules by which it is played must be as great as the abilities of all the players. In housing this means that there must be as many opportunities to carry out decisions as there are decisions demanded. Large productive organizations and their designers do not meet these rules of fair play. But the system of resourcefulness does.

Resourcefulness requires imagination, initiative, and above all personal will, which are fairly consistent and evenly distributed human qualities. A householder's determination to invest time, effort, and skill in his and her home and surroundings depends on the satisfaction they can expect from the usefulness of their housing.

Architects and designers for the most part are gentlemen and ladies of culture, retained by large productive organizations. Their education and their professional skills are developed to plan for the production and consumption of manufactured products. They are experts on the rules of the game of industrial design and have been able to play by their rules for they own the ball.

However, designers find it difficult to comprehend the rules and principles of the game of resourcefulness which are based on the spontaneous recognition of the use of materials and opportunities generated not by sale but by use. The two are simply games with different rules and different reasons for playing, like polo and stickball. However, they both have one characteristic in common, fair play.

To ignore or even worse to condemn the imaginative struggle for survival of squatters because of the ugliness of poverty is not only poor sportsmanship, but it rules designers, planners, and architects out of the game. It relegates professional designers to the sidelines of what may well be the most important design game of our time. Squatter handicapping cannot compare to the games played at Monte Carlo, Las Vegas, or Suffolk Downs, and industrial designers do not own the ball, but the game is infinitely more exciting and the stakes infinitely higher.

choice as science

Systems and systems-thinking, as it has been used, tends to remove decisions further from the work place and center them in higher echelons of management. This is not the inevitable result of the search for rational methods in design. A theory to free the client from the "patronage" of the architect and simultaneously render the architect useful to the client has been proposed and used by architect Yona Friedman, under the heading of "scientific architecture."[15]

"What can we know and how can we know it?" Friedman asks. The client describes his specific needs to the architect. The architect devotes a great deal of time to gathering the specific information necessary to make the client's needs clear in his mind. How much time would one architect require to understand the needs of ten thousand clients? This would take more time than the five thousand years that compose the written history of humankind. Yet we consistently consider it quite reasonable for one architect to design for ten thousand users. This, says Friedman, is not only unscientific, but immoral.

There are two solutions to this problem and both present difficulties. The first is to supply enough designers so that they can devote themselves to each user, one at a time, which would mean that there were as many designers as there were people in the world, perhaps more. The second solution is to reduce the time needed to gather information. Since it is impossible to find the specific needs of each user, an effort is made to find the average needs of all users. But the average does not exist. Therefore, the needs of unreal users are designed for and the system ends in discomfort.

We do know that the architect and planner design buildings and parts of towns and cities which must satisfy two criteria. We know the first concerns physical properties in which the elements used in the design of buildings and city parts are produced by manufacturers, artisans, and human labor. Secondly, the designer selects appropriate products from catalogs and assembles them. The second activity, termed "design," is considered the important part of the architect's work. The designer gives instructions to others on how the parts are assembled through the medium of plans and specifications. Eventually, a building or town or city part is realized from these instructions.

INSTALLATION OF METAL CURTAIN WALL
NEW YORK CITY, 1963

THE WORLD TRADE CENTER, NEW YORK CITY, FROM GOVERNOR'S ISLAND

The individual builds his dwelling

The craftsman helps the individual build

The architect is intermediary between the craftsman and the individual

JOHN HABRAKEN DIVIDED THE RELATIONSHIP BETWEEN USER AND DESIGNER INTO SEVEN CATEGORIES AS SHOWN HERE. THE FIRST SIX OF THESE FALL WITHIN YONA FRIEDMAN'S FIRST THREE INFORMATION SYSTEMS. THE SEVENTH, A NON-RELATIONSHIP IS WHAT YONA FRIEDMAN HAS TERMED THE SHORT-CIRCUIT.

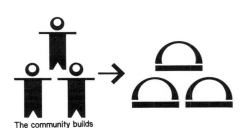

The community builds

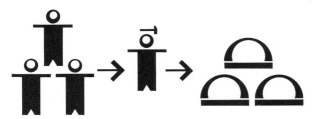

The craftsman helps the community build

The architect is intermediary between the craftsman and the community

The designer has arranged the parts to satisfy the client's objectives, and, in most instances, never has any contact at all with the user of his or her designs. In designing for anonymous users, criteria can again be organized into two distinct categories.

We know that the first is the use of "objective" criteria, which concerns the efficiency of the designed product as used. This efficiency has no relation to the user's taste, culture, religion, or opinions. For example, a wall is always an obstacle to passage and an opening permits passage through the wall. This is true in any culture, country, or society. Passage or nonpassage is an objective criterion.

We know that the second category, which can be called "aesthetic" criteria, is more difficult to define. Values change with individual taste, culture, religion, and opinion for each individual user. The individual users who are not known individually to the designer nonetheless consider themselves individuals, and it is this individuality that must be satisfied.

It is evident that if objective criteria are satisfied and aesthetic criteria are not, the designed object might still be efficient in use, even though it might be considered nonaesthetic by some users. On the other hand, if the objective criteria are not satisfied, the object is not efficient in use, whether considered aesthetic or not. In this instance, although aesthetic criteria are acceptable to a majority of the users, the object designed might cause damage to them. Under the best of circumstances, the object can be considered sculpture; under the worst, a dangerous obstruction.

It is clear then that the first priority must be given to objective criteria. Aesthetic criteria are discretional. The task that Yona Friedman has set himself in the formulation of a scientific architecture is to implement a method in which objective and aesthetic criteria can be satisfied. Obviously, the method cannot be one of trial and error, since human beings are the raw material of the experiment.

The method Friedman has devised is simply one of disclosure of objective criteria that can be known and leaves the selection of aesthetic criteria, which is known differently to every user, to the user's discretion. Friedman's goal is to implement a method which will eliminate information short circuits and unreliability from the message on arrival to the user and to find means that will inform the user of the dangers or consequences of their selections.

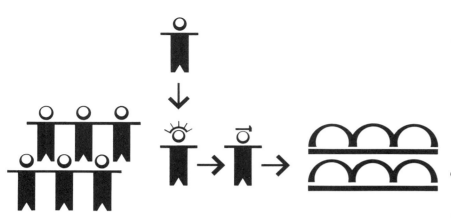

A non-relationship a specialist tells the architect who directs
the craftsman in building mass housing

THE NON-RELATIONSHIP AND THE SHORT-CIRCUIT

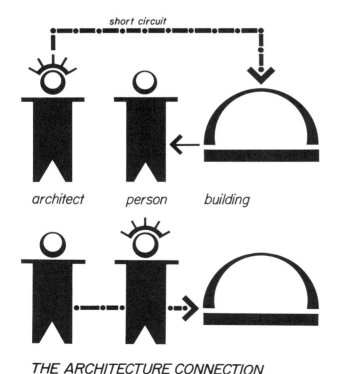

architect   person   building

THE ARCHITECTURE CONNECTION

Short circuits in the information system must be eliminated.
There are four information systems:

1. The user builds and the information is self-contained.
2. The builder is instructed by the user.
3. The user instructs the architect, who instructs the builder.
4. The architect translates the fictitious choices of an
    average person to a builder.

It is in this fourth relationship that the short circuit
occurs.

Friedman's solution proposes to restore the direct
relationship of the user to the designed object, even though
there are innumerable users. The skills of the designer are
utilized to implement the desires of the user, rather than
frustrate them through the medium of a fictitious third person.

The user is to be given a repertoire, which of necessity would
be limited, of all the possible arrangements of solutions that his
or her way of life would require. This repertoire must be presented
in a form the user could understand. There must also be a warning
connected to each choice, again phrased in terms the user can comprehend. The warning will acquaint the user with the advantages and
disadvantages of the user's selection.

Warnings cannot be based on a particular value system, but must
be based on the intrinsic properties, the objective criteria, and
the objective logic of the solution. It is entirely possible that
the same warning may represent an advantage to one user and in incon-
venience or even danger to another, since the two users may have
entirely different ways of life.

The users must inform themselves by means of the repertoire
and select an item from the list and then explain the use
directly to the artisan who will produce the building. It is
the user who takes responsibility for the entire process, since
he or she has been warned of the implications of the particular
solution chosen. The architect has not been eliminated, but
the role changed. The designer constructs the repertoire.

The telephone system can be used as an example of such a
repertoire. Any ten digits is a potential telephone number.
The telephone directory is the warning. It warns anyone who
wants to use the telephone by informing them of the consequences
of the act by telling them who will answer the call. The
infrastructure, the technical network, when constructed properly,
will route all calls from any one station to any other.

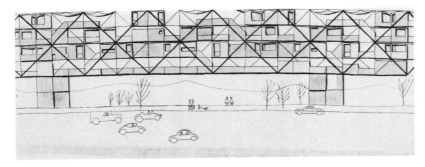

DESIGNS FOR AN ARCHITECTURE OF CHOICE BY YONA FRIEDMAN. AN
INFRA STRUCTURE OF CITY SERVICES SUPPORTS HOUSING OF
THE OWNER'S SELECTION. (Drawings by Yona Friedman)

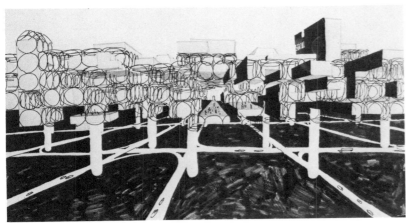

Those who build the telephone and service it are not obliged
to tell the one using the telephone who they should speak to or
what they should say. The infrastructure is therefore impersonal.
The telephone indicates how a highly technical and impersonal system
can be used to express the most personal feelings of the people who
will use it. Cities are constructed over highly technical and
impersonal systems of plumbing, electrical, and transportation
services, which are very much the same; yet London, New York, Tokyo,
and Calcutta are entirely different and individual cities.

The essence of Friedman's proposal is simply that the act of
deciding implies with it that the one who makes the decision is the
one who takes the risks. Any system that does not give the right
of choice to those who must bear the consequence of bad decisions
is immoral. To change the immoral situation that now exists Friedman
has searched for a method that will guarantee the user the power of
decision, after the user thoroughly understands the risks involved.
It is both immoral and dangerous to leave choices to people who have
not been properly informed of the consequences of their decisions.

The future user and designer must share the same skills.
Both must know how to read the repertoire, how to make choices
from it, and how to heed the warnings. These skills could be
taught in primary school. The designer will merely need more
skill than the user, which could be learned in the university.
The method is familiar in the teaching of mathematics. The
mathematician and the layman use the same set of symbols--plus,
minus, multiplication, and division--but at different levels
of complexity. An understanding is possible between them.

A restaurant menu is another example of a user repertoire.
The menu describes the dish and its price. The stomach and
the purse are warned. The menu lists all the dishes available
by name and description of how the food will be prepared. The
diner reads the menu, is informed, and can compare this information against previous experience. When a meal or combination
of dishes is presented, no two people may select the same
combination even though they dine together. A meal is a
matter of personal choice. There is no independent scale of
values that says one gastronomical composition is better than
another either in absolute or other scale of values. The
owner of the restaurant and the cook do not agree or disagree
with the patron if the choice disagrees with their own taste
or even if they feel the bill will be extravagant. Their
function is to serve the patron whatever is ordered from the
repertoire and in accordance with the information the menu
contains. The creative work of the restaurant owner consists

of arranging the menu and the creative work of the cook in preparing the food.

Friedman proposes as complete a list of all choices as possible that the user can comprehend and is free to choose any possible combinations, instead of accepting the preferences and tastes of the designer. The cost is the warning.

The profession that arranges the repertoire and the instructions for its use must do so scientifically and practice a teachable discipline, Friedman maintains. This is the new version of the designer, architect, and planner that emerges from another view of professional activity and responsibility.

footnotes

1. Edward de Bono – THE MECHANISM OF MIND, Pelican (Penguin), Baltimore, Md., 1971 (p. 151).
2. Richard Bender – Conversations with F. Wilson, North Hampton, 1969.
3. N. J. Habraken – A synopsis of views expressed by Habraken in SUPPORTS, Praeger Paperbacks, N.Y.C., 1972 – INTERBUILD, Oct., 1967 (pp. 12-19) – THREE R's FOR HOUSING, originally published in Forum (Holland) Vol. xx n. 1, December, 1966 – PLAN, Holland 1970, The Pursuit of an Ides (p. 160).
4. Pacific Domes – DOMEBOOK ONE, DOMEBOOK TWO, Las Gatos, California, Portola Institute, Santa Cruz, California, 1970.
5. DOMUS, December, 1975; September, 1976; Milan, Italy, (p. 30).
6. See p. 8.
7. Richard Bender – Conversations with F. Wilson, Clothing as Shelter, South Hampton, L.I., 1968.
8. Robert Probst – Progressive Architecture, Nov., 1974. (pp. 80-81).
9. Herbert Read – 'THE MEANING OF ART, Pelican, Penguin Books in association with Faber and Faber, Harmondsworth, Middlesex, England, 1931.
10. Melvyn Kaufman – Conversations with F. Wilson, Views of the Owner Builder, 1966-1973.
11. Mark Gimson, Caroline Lwin and Nick Wates – SQUATTING, THE FOURTH ARM OF HOUSING?, Architectural Design, April, 1976 (p. 211).
12. William Mangin and John C. Turner – THE BARRIADA MOVEMENT, Progressive Architecture, May, 1968. Also included are ideas expressed by Turner at CIDOC, Cuernavaca, 1970 and in his book HOUSING BY PEOPLE, Pantheon Books, N.Y.C., 1976.
13. Geoffrey K. Payne – FUNCTIONS OF INFORMALITY, A Case Study of Squatters Settlements in India, Architectural Design, August, 1973 (p. 494).
14. Paul Andrews, Malcolm Christis, Richard Martin – SQUATTERS, And The Evolution Of A Lifestyle, Architectural Design, January, 1973.
15. Yona Friedman – TOWARD A SCIENTIFIC ARCHITECTURE, MIT Press, Cambridge, Mass., 1977.

cHoIce ChOIcE cₕ⬤icE CHoi7e chOiCE
CHOiCE ChⵔiCE cHoIcE CHoICe CHoiCe
CₕHoiCe CₕOICE ⵔhOicE cHOicE CHⵔiCe
ChOice Cholⵔe CholCE cHoicⵔ cHoiⵔe
Chⵔicⵔ CₕHOIce chOice cHOiⵔ CHolcE
CHⵔICe cHOicE ChOice ChⵔiCe CHoicE
cHo!Ce ⵔhⵔIce CHoICE CHolcE Chⵔice
ChOIcE ⵔHoiCe CHoicE Cₕolce

"I am an expert on myself" signed **POGO POSSUM**

Conclusion

"The urgent problem of our time is that of transforming a million slum dwellings into cities of light, order, health, and convenience." Herbert Read wrote this before it was recognized that the problem was not a million, but millions, and it was still believed that industrial designers could be entrusted with such a task. It has since become painfully evident that the institutions the designers perpetuate are themselves part of the problem.

Yet there is a crucial need for design. One is to give form to communal decisions. The other is that of recognizing and nourishing the vital self-generating growths that have taken root in the interstices of our moribund indifferent monolithic economic, production, and social systems.

Designers will be useful if they learn to see the act of building as Hassan Fathy described it while rehousing the tomb robbers of Gourna.

> *Building is a creative activity in which the decisive moment is the instant of conception, that instant when the spirit takes shape and all the features of the new creation are virtually determined. While all the characteristics of a living creature are irrevocably settled at the moment of fertilization, the characteristics of a building are determined by the whole complex of decisions made by everyone that has a say in the matter, at every stage of its construction. Thus the instant of conception on which the final form of a living creature rests becomes for a building a multiplicity of such instants, each playing a decisive part in the total creative process.*
>
> *If we can identify and seize these instants, then we can control the whole process of creation.*[1]

What Fathy described is the multifaceted spontaneous design of ordinary people. This is entirely different than industrial design, which has only one unshared creative moment. Creativity in industrial design is the sole province of the designer who covetously guards every aspect of it solely as his or her possession.

KING OF THE MOUNTAIN
(Courtesy of Gilda and Vic Bonardi)

SEARS TOWER CHICAGO, SKIDMORE, OWINGS AND MERRILL
ARCHITECTS (Photo by Ezra Stoller courtesy of
Skidmore, Owings and Merrill)

The academies that train designers, the professional organizations that guard their privileges, and the government agencies that license their right to practice all jealously guard the designer's monopoly of creativity and exclude the right of anyone else to exercise this right. If designers are to change, it will mean change in their education, professional associations, and government agencies.

One way that such change may be stimulated is to recognize that all building has the possibility of becomine architecture, and the moments of creativity that Fathy described can be acknowledged and encouraged wherever they occur. It creative building is the common denominator of architecture, squatters can be recognized as competent planners for devising means of living in high densities on land that planners discard. Scrounged-material builders can be lauded for engineering feats with dump materials that engineers disdain. Suburbanites can be admired as the last dillitante interior designers, architects, and landscape architects.

The designer's task will remain that of giving form to those structures that the community wishes to expend the resources and energy to have designed. These are public buildings--city halls, churches, bowling alleys, and car washes--in which the activities that take place are not of great importance. But the designer's task can also be enlarged to encompass that of finding ways to realize the moments of creativity Fathy describes in the act of people making themselves comfortable in the world. Here the living functions are terribly important; so important that designers cannot design them.

Designers must find ways to encourage creativity where the only resources are the will, the energy, and the ingenuity of the user. This is their great challenge. To accomplish this it is necessary to ignore the artificial distinction between the will to form of the fine artist and the will to form of those not trained in the academies.

A famous artist once said, "If an artist spits, it is art." We know that artistic spit cannot be distinguished from ordinary spit on the city sidewalk. Spitting and creativity are universal human attributes and not the exclusive characteristic of individuals called "artists." In fact, only an artist would confuse the two. The difference between artistic and ordinary spit is only of academic interest. It is much less confusing to identify spit as spit and art as art, no matter who does either.

ENTRANCE TO FUJI GROUP PAVILION, OSAKA WORLDS FAIR, 1970
WINDOW GRATING, NEW GOURNA

Hassan Fathy in building a city of light, order, health, and convenience, using mud brick, discovered another role for the professional very much akin to the original definition. The architect that Fathy became was one in whom the professional's life was the testimonial to what he professed. The cruciality of the task was found in sharing the designer's knowledge and encouraging creativity in all the moments of building, as Fathy did with his Nubian masons. Gourna was a village that grew. The fact that its forms were fine examples of the art of building was a by-product. Architecture was not the object of building, but the natural result. The useful architect will have to understand building, as well as the medieval Master Mason, but, more importantly, will have to learn to do as Eric Hoffer did on the docks of San Francisco--learn to praise well.

This is not a question of choice for the industrial designers who call themselves "architects." Architects, although their skills have never been more needed and despite the proud title, are of little importance in today's world. In the design act of materializing culture for institutional clients the art of architecture has become as frivolous, snobbish, and ludicrous as any of the other "fine arts." Architects are simply stylists whose work does little good and little harm and provides a certain amount of entertainment.

But the art of building as part of the great upheaval of our time, reaching toward autonomy as a reaction against the mindless restrictions and work patterns imposed upon us by moribund bureaucracies, is another matter entirely.

Building in all its aspects, from squatter settlements to the Maryland suburbs, is not only survival, it is a medium for attaining dignity, self-directed freedom, and moral independence. In freeing perceptions, exercising judgment, expressing the universal will to form of all people, building is an essential, joyful, unpredictable, vital human activity. For if humans do not build, they die.

For designers who have grown beyond catering to the divine right of kings and institutions to the tending to the growth of the design right of ordinary people, the creative possibilities know no bounds.

footnotes

1. Hassan Fathy - ARCHITECTURE FOR THE POOR - University of Chicago Press, Chicago, London, 1973 (p. 22).

DWELLING ENTRANCE, ATLANTA, GEORGIA
(Photo by F. Wilson)

When a man's house ceases to be built he dies

ANCIENT PERSIAN SAYING

KILROY AS THE EGYPTIAN WINGED BAT
(A spirit that symbolized the physical
survival of the dead by which they
returned to their haunts in the
mortal world.)

WINDOW OF ORIENTAL GROCERY STORE (Photo by Richard Jones)

Bibliography

WORK AND TECHNOLOGY

Harry Braverman - LABOR AND MONOPOLY CAPITAL, Monthly Review Press, N.Y.C., 1974

Karl Marx - CAPITAL, Modern Library, N.Y.C., 1906

Milton Meltzer - SLAVERY: FROM THE RISE OF WESTERN CIVILIZATION TO TODAY, Dell, N.Y.C., 1971

National Commission on Product Safety - FINAL REPORT OF THE NATIONAL COMMISSION ON PRODUCT SAFETY, U.S. Government Printing Office, Washington D.C., 1970

Martin Pawley - GARBAGE HOUSING, Architectural Review Press, London, 1975

Report of Special Task Force to the Secretary of HEW - WORK IN AMERICA, MIT, Cambridge, Massachusetts, 1973

Studs Terkel - WORKING, Avon, N.Y.C., 1972

Alexis de Tocqueville - DEMOCRACY IN AMERICA, VOLUMES I and 2, Vintage, N.Y.C., 1945

Eileen Yeo and E. P. Thompson - THE UNKNOWN MAYHEW, Schocken, N.Y.C., 1971

DESIGN AND DESIGN THEORY

Ulrich Conrads - PROGRAMS AND MANIFESTOES ON 20TH-CENTURY ARCHITECTURE, MIT, Cambridge, Massachusetts, 1970

Le Corbusier - TOWARDS A NEW ARCHITECTURE, Praeger, N.Y.C., 1960

Le Corbusier - THE CITY OF TOMORROW, MIT, Cambridge, Massachusetts, 1971

Horatio Greenough - FORM AND FUNCTION, University of California Press, Berkeley, 1962

Walter Gropius - SCOPE OF TOTAL ARCHITECTURE, Collier, N.Y.C., 1961

Nicholas Negroponte - THE ARCHITECTURE MACHINE, MIT, Cambridge, Massachusetts, 1970

George Nelson - PROBLEMS OF DESIGN, Whitney, N.Y.C., 1957

Paul Overy - DE STIJL, Studio Vista, London, 1969

Herbert Read - THE MEANING OF ART, Pelican, Baltimore, Md., 1949

Herbert Read - THE PHILOSOPHY OF MODERN ART, Meridian, N.Y.C., 1954

Herbert Read - ART AND INDUSTRY, Indiana University Press, Bloomington, Indiana, 1961

Wilhelm Worringer - FORM IN GOTHIC, Schocken, N.Y.C., 1964

HISTORY AND TECHNOLOGY

Richard Bender - A CRACK IN THE REAR VIEW MIRROR, Van Nostrand Reinhold, N.Y.C., 1970

Siegfried Giedion - MECHANIZATION TAKES COMMAND, Norton, N.Y.C., 1969

John A. Kouwenhoven - THE ARTS IN MODERN AMERICAN CIVILIZATION, Norton, N.Y.C., 1948

Melvin Kranzberg and Joseph Gies - BY THE SWEAT OF THY BROW, Putnam, N.Y.C., 1975

Gary T. Moore, Ed. - EMERGING METHODS IN ENVIRONMENTAL DESIGN AND PLANNING, MIT, Cambridge, Massachusetts, 1968

GENERAL HISTORY

Gordon Childe - WHAT HAPPENED IN HISTORY, Pelican, Baltimore, Md., 1942

Howard W. Haggard, M.D. - DEVILS, DRUGS AND DOCTORS, Pocket Books, N.Y.C., 1946

Charles Jencks - MODERN MOVEMENTS IN ARCHITECTURE, Doubleday, Garden City, N.Y., 1971

Nicolaus Pevsner - AN OUTLINE OF EUROPEAN ARCHITECTURE, Pelican, Baltimore, Md., 1945

Nicolaus Pevsner - PIONEERS OF MODERN DESIGN, Pelican, Baltimore, Md., 1960

HOUSING AND ARCHITECTURE

Charles Abrams - THE CITY IS THE FRONTIER, Harper Colophon, N.Y.C., 1965

Hassan Fathy - GOURNA A TALE OF TWO VILLAGES, Ministry of Culture, Cairo, Egypt, 1969

Yona Friedman - TOWARD A SCIENTIFIC ARCHITECTURE, MIT, Cambridge, Ma., 1975

John Habraken - SUPPORTS, Praeger, N.Y.C., 1972

John Habraken - AAP NOOT MIES HUIS, Amsterdam, Netherlands, 1966

J. M. Richards - THE CASTLES ON THE GROUND, John Murray, London, 1973

John F. C. Turner - HOUSING BY PEOPLE, Pantheon, N.Y.C., 1976

THE NATURE OF DESIGN

Edward de Bono - THE MECHANISM OF MIND, Pelican, Baltimore, Md., 1969

Ivan Illich - TOOLS FOR CONVIVIALITY, Perennial Library, N.Y.C., 1973

David Pye - THE NATURE OF DESIGN, Van Nostrand Reinhold, N.Y.C., 1964

THE NATURE OF PROFESSIONS

Editors of Daedalus - THE PROFESSIONS IN AMERICA, Beacon, Boston, 1963

Laurence B. Holland - WHO DESIGNS AMERICA?, Anchor, Garden City, N.Y., 1966

Index

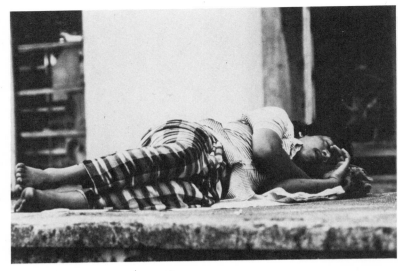

(Courtesy of Dhairu Thadani)